SOS
Surviving
Suicide

Judge on *Channel 4* 'The Great Pottery Throw Down

"Dean had a vision for a collection of work that was not about the poets or the egos of particular artists, but about honest raw responses to a mental health crisis. A book that could perhaps make somebody think, somebody stop or save a life."
–Carlotta Allum, Director, *Stretch* in the Foreword

Nirala Series

SOS : Surviving Suicide

Dean Stalham is a British artist, poet and writer currently living in Margate in the UK. Since leaving prison Dean has written and produced a number of plays to critical acclaim. Dean has always been a campaigner for the arts and its ability to give people a voice. He founded the charity Art Saves Lives and recently worked with *Stretch* as a curator and project coordinator creating a platform for Outsider Art. Dean is currently writing a book and is regularly sponsored by the Arts Council in England. Dean is a published poet and this project came from his desire to use the format to say something about people in these difficult times.

SOS

Surviving

Suicide

a collection of poems
that may save a life

Editor

Dean Stalham

Foreword by
Carlotta Allum
of *Stretch*

Nirala

Nirala Publications
4637/20, Third Floor, 310, Hari Sadan,
Ansari Road, Daryaganj,
New Delhi 110 002
www.niralapublications.com
niralabooks@yahoo.co.in

———

First Edition 2021

———

ISBN: 978-81-951915-1-2

———

Copyright© Dean Stalham & Contributors

———

Cover Design : Tarun Saxena/Graphical House

Printed at
Chaman Offset Press
New Delhi-110092

Foreword

This collection of poems is an important piece of work. I have worked alongside Dean Stalham for the last eight years trying to provide opportunities and give a voice to artists who are trying to do something meaningful with their work and may not have a platform. When I heard about the idea for this project, I really wanted STRETCH, my charity, to give it full support and validation as in these urgent times the issue of mental health and suicide has never been more pertinent.

The interest and the feedback for the project has been overwhelming, suicide prevention charities vulnerable groups and people who are reaching out in these dark times. These poems should be in every student library and sitting with every group charity for people to read.

Dean had a vision for a collection of work that was not about the poets or the egos of particular artists, but about honest raw responses to a mental health crisis. A book that could perhaps make somebody think, somebody stop or save a life.

— Carlotta Allum
www.stretch-charity.org

'All I know is -
I will never see
my beautiful boys smile again'

RIP Mark Cleasey A.K.A Naturalbornquiller

Contents

SOS
Surviving
Suicide

Mark Cleasey was a leading London performance poet. Although severely dyslexic, against all the odds he never failed to get his work and words out there. He was also a hero. He was present at THE BRIXTON BOMBING on April 17th 1999. Although injured by the nail bomb himself he was instrumental in getting people out safely from harms way. He was also a Director of The Anti Knife Crime Charity and movement 'Saving Our Boys and Girls' and led a march to Downing Street to raise issues of teenage knife crime and its victims.

One day he left his home and travelled to a park where he played as a child. It was there that Mark Cleasey took his own life.

On Earth Mark was a shining star as I am sure he is in the heavens.

--Editor

IVE BEEN ALONE BEFORE
But NOT liKE this
IVE lost A lot
DRY EYES ARE WHAT I Miss
DAYS AND DAYS IVE WONDERD
life and loved ONES IVE
PONDERD
a lonley life im in
Can t Seem to get out
all along With thoughts
THE WRONG RoNg i Have
Wonder D.
PackEd My Bags and Said
good Bye, to love friends
and family

RAVI SHANKAR

The Great Sun

"...and then, I have nature and art and poetry, and if that is not enough, what is enough?"
– Vincent Willem van Gogh

Originally worshipped within moveable paper-thin walls
of a Shingon Buddhist temple from Heian Period Japan

that burned down, somehow, in ensuing rain squalls,
the sculpture made completely of wood had a lifespan

more to live, for it survived and was stored on a farm,
before being bought by a museum behind which I crumpled

on the pavement the first time I contemplated self-harm.
I had been vilified on the evening news, was in trouble

with the law and my marriage was disintegrating. I hated
myself mainly, and wanted to sink into a soundless void

where shame has no voice. The hurt could not be located
in my body, nor my mind. Instead, all I wanted to avoid

grew into a forest of strangler figs filled with whispers.
Everywhere I turned, gnarled branches gripped the sky

in fists. I wanted to vanish. Luckily there are two figures
in this tableau. There's someone whose love can indemnify

infamy, who will hold me curled as a comma in the womb
of a novel bound to be pulped. She took me into triage

in the emergency room, else I could have been entombed
by the wish to die. Was the week I spent in treatment a mirage

or was it the blind life I thought I was living in plain sight?
Locked in the chamber of a Tudor-Gothic hospital, I prayed

and wept, slept and delayed contacting my family. Fight
or flight and I had chosen the latter. Depressed, upbraided,

scared and on medication, I did not know where to turn.
Then suddenly I remembered the Buddha, DainichiNyorai,

the Great Sun, the generative force that can either burn
or nourish. The wood of the sculpture glows warm, its eye

penetrates yours, until the obsessive needs of self-narration
stops. I stopped. I needed to stop. I needed to eat green jello,

color and sit in a circle without judgement or expectation
with people who normally I would not even have said hello

to. Who cares if I were a Professor? All titles and names
dropped away and I remembered what it meant to breathe

freely again. Listen, there's always hope. Ignore those claims
otherwise. If you dig deep enough, there's love underneath

trauma and a Buddha-view from which, being just a grain
of sand in a mandala, whether yellow ochre, red sandstone

or crushed gypsum, the winds can sweep away mortal pain
and scatter fear in the cosmic vastness of all that's unknown.

dPART

Rope

Sitting on this park bench always reminiscing
Mind constantly drifting to the day I nearly did it
Sometimes I wish it happened, wont publicly admit
But these are the thoughts trapped in the mind of a cynic
Thought that nobody could help me
Not a doctor or a clinic
Whether a rope of or some bills these bad thoughts they could have ridden
But I'm glad that they didn't that would have only passed the pain on
Look in the mirror see my demons now I tell them thats is game on
On what I thought was my final day I thought about my family
How would my wife supports my kids without the help of my salary
Thought about how my son would handle all the questions
Would it lead him down the wrong path to doing drugs or getting arrested
Would my wife find another man and would they go on to call him dad
These thoughts are to much I can't give in ill give it all I have
I have to stay strong what I show has to be grit
The truth is I didn't stop myself my family did
R is for recovery I really hope I stay sane
O is for 'oh my god' some people cope with the same pain
P is for perseverance so many perish but they ain't named
E is for the energy I need to get me through the day
Put em all together it's the tool for an exit
But I'm glad that I didn't. I'm glad I didn't end it.

BANU ERCON

That Day

When I sat down that day, and looked at my life,
Emptiness, sadness, no future or fight.
I tried to think, of reasons to stay,
Surely someone would regret my actions that day.

All I knew, is that I hated myself,
I could see the disgust in those eyes around me.
Thirteen years old, and no future to think of,
No-one who understands, no-one to turn to.

I stared at the pills, I'd been saving them for weeks,
This was my time, this was my destiny.
I started to fade, I feel calm and free,
The pain was over, I could fly now and sleep.

When I woke up it was chaos, being dragged from my bed,
Ending up in the hospital, stomach pumped, not dead.
That was my first thought, when I woke up from my haze,
I'm so useless and pathetic, I will live another day.

I could not believe, that I had failed again,
Nothing I did, was successful or great.
Such a basic thing, that I had to do,
Just to end my life, and the pain for those around me too.

I'd like to say that was the end of my struggle,
But life has been eventful, and I've tried to stay humble.
At forty-three years, I still think about the ending,
How easy it would be, how I could stop pretending.

But life can be beautiful, and moments can change you,
Love and warmth, can sometimes protect you.
So I fight for each day, with hopeful enthusiasm,
Breathe in, breathe out, one foot in front of the other.

If all else fails,
I'll hold on for tomorrow,
Fresh hope with each sunrise,
For a bright new day.

DANIELLE BUTTERS

I nearly said goodbye

It was the day
I nearly said goodbye
I picked up the drink and started to cry
I walked to the edge
My last place to sleep
These thoughts in my head just won't keep
Some pills to ease my pain
Weather was perfect it just started to rain
I laid on the floor
The rain hurt my face
But I closed my eyes once more
Then I saw a light, I felt a hand of my friend
She told me this isn't the end
She took me inside
And made me be sick
The pills didn't work she got there so quick
I didn't think things would get better
They did
talking to people Helped me live
My life only got brighter
I came to have three shining stars
My children who lift up my world beyond Mars
The pain comes and goes

But I know I can fight
I can see the day turn to night
I can talk I am needed I am loved
If only they know what I know now
I've felt the pain of losing someone this way now
My brother
In silence he would suffer
Pushed us away one way or another
He took the pain away but it stabbed me inside iv never felt a
pain like that ever in my life
There is a piece missing a hole in my heart it will never mend
To not be able to say goodbye or stop him ill always comprehend
To clear his bedroom where he laid himself to rest
To have my sisters cry on my chest
To never hear him sing a song
Or tell me what I did wrong
The pain is nothing like no other
So please keep fighting for another
For your family
For your friends
Be honest say how you feel
These emotions are real
Lets stand together for mental health
And learn to love ourself

CHRISTOPHER SOUTHGATE

Sestina
for Karen and Ros and Sue, Richard and Peter and Simon,
and many others

I came here when I was nineteen, to get well
from a kind of flash-flood of down, from a tyrant rule
of spiders over the thin moon of me. Safe from harm
here, they said. The film'll run slowly. Under control.
No-one will have to know. No-one will notice.
They didn't say I'd come out with a label.

Mind you, it was a kind of comfort, the label,
at first. People could see I'd fallen down a well
that was real. It made them take notice.
Then we lost our insurance. It's a rule,
the girl on the phone said. So I lost control
and broke the phone. My friend left. Only then the self-harm

and the Seclusion Room. What's the harm,
I said, if I cut myself? Is that the wrong label?
They tried things out till I was under control:
Thirty milligrams the spiders. Seventy milligrams, well,
Numbness, like living yesterday over. Fifty mgs rule
O.K. Not disruptive enough to notice.

I watch the trees a lot. I stand by the notice
That says all visitors must sign in and out. Harm-
less words. I tell another patient it's a good rule.
He tells me I'm a police spy. I like that label.
Whoever made my loneliness made it well.
But who was it? And is he still in control?

Sometimes I stand and think - this is a sick plan to control
a special person who's been fighting stuff a long time. 'Notice
the difference, when you treat me right!' I shout. Does no harm.
It is better here, than years ago. Same label -
but they ask about the colour of the bricks in your well.
Sometimes they help you choose to go ahead and keep a rule.

Maybe it has to be that certain drugs rule
your life, that without them there's just no control
over the downs. But staff do talk to you, go past the label,
if you get the right one, with some time to notice
you. To see you're choosing between living and no more harm
ever again. I read once that all shall be well -

tell me then: if I knew every rule, and could get people to notice
me, and was under control with the drugs, and was no harm
to anyone, and lost my label, would I be called well?

*Commissioned by the local NHS Trust to express the concerns of long-term
sufferers of mental illness, and read in the Service held in Exeter Cathedral
to mark 50 years of the NHS in Devon.*

ROY BARKER

I have a choice

Suicide is such a lonely death
Unhappy you decided to take your last breath
Regardless of the loved ones you left behind
Victim of the demons in your mind
I had a choice --give up or survive
Valuing your memories has kept me alive
Often I thought of joining you too
Raging at what you were putting me through
Screaming, yelling and crying for you
One day my storm calmed I could see the light
Family and friends helped me start my fight
So my memories start to come swirling round
Unexpected thoughts of you start to abound
I hear your voice, your laughter your fears
Causing me to smile then burst into tears
I have a choice to love you or hate you
Drifting from one to the other I do
Enduring the lonely empty ache left by you

BENJAMIN ZEPHANIAH

You can hold your head high

If you can keep your money when governments about you
Are losing theirs and blaming it on you,
If you can trust your neighbour when they trust not you
And they be very nosy too;
If you can await the warm delights of summer
Then summer comes and goes with sun not seen,
And pay so much for drinking water
Knowing that the water is unclean.

If you seek peace in times of war creation,
And you can see that oil merchants are to blame,
If you can meet a pimp or politician,
And treat those two impostors just the same;
If you cannot bear dis-united nations
And you think dis new world order is a trick,
If you've ever tried to build good race relations,
And watch bad policing mess your work up quick.

If you can make one heap of all your savings
And risk buying a small house and a plot,
Then sit back and watch the economy inflating
Then have to deal with the negative equity you've got;
If you can force your mind and body to continue

When all the social services have gone,
If you struggle on when there is nothing in you,
Except the knowledge that justice cannot be wrong.

If you can speak the truth to common people
Or walk with Kings and Queens and live no lie,
If you can see how power can be evil
And know that every censor is a spy;
If you can fill an unforgiving lifetime
With years of working hard to make ends meet,
You may not be wealthy but I am sure you will find
That you can hold your head high as you walk the streets.

The Angry Black Poet

Next on stage
We have the angry black poet,
So angry
He won't allow himself to fall in luv,
So militant
You will want to see him again.
Don't get me wrong
He means it,
He means it so much
He is unable to feel,
He's so serious
If he is found smiling
He stops to get serious before he enters stage left,
Through days he dreams of freedom
Through nights he rants of freedom,
Tonight he will speak for you,
Give him a hand.

Please give him a hand,
Help him,
He too has silent moments
He could do without,
I have worked with him
And I know
He needs stroking
He needs to play
Let him know you are there.

I knew him when he was unknown
I knew him when he was happy,
Now he's angry
You will luv him,
He lives on the edge
He has highs and lows

And I know
He hates publicity
And he luvs you all,
Be quiet
And let's hear it for
The angry black poet.

TIM TOMLINSON

Multiple Attempts on Dark Hollow Road, Friday Nights in Winter

(for Tommy Walters)

The way you drove in snowstorms, the way
the tires lost their grip at the bend the way

we spun and spun and spun right into
oncoming cars the way you laughed that laugh

that laugh that crossed between scream
and manifesto and the way that

drivers in the oncoming cars panicked
the way they honked their horns and flashed

their brights and cut their wheels the way
they raised their arms as if those might stop

you coming on and on and on. And the way
we spun right past them every time

right on past them every time and coasted down
to Main Street at the hill's bottom and swung

a U and turned back up Liberty Avenue
to do it again. And the way you rejoiced, pounding

the steering wheel, shouting, "Did you see
his fucking face!" which of course I did—

the sheer terror, the split-second awareness
that this time was the time and how there was

never enough time to get it all together,
to get it all in order to prepare for this time,

this exact time that he knew was coming,
knew all along was coming, the way we all know

that it's coming, we know it all the time.
What he couldn't know was how perfectly

you were in control. Every time. How could he?
How could you? How could I?

Last Words

for Wesley G.

Something is missing.
I don't feel fulfilled,
and a man should feel fulfilled.
Sated—
the way you feel after catfish and mud pie.

It's not about having children, numerous lovers.
It's not about career,

how many books,
none of that.

It's about delivering a message.
And I haven't delivered a message.
I don't even know what my message is.

Godless

I have no relationship with God but
he's never held that against me. He gives
me the rain, and Rilke, and sweet mangoes.
He gives me coffee and the chamber music

of Ravel. Sometimes I wake up from dreams
shaking my head over something clearly
put there by something not myself, something
entirely outside my experience.

I stand in the refrigerator's light.
I think, yes, but then, no. I move a magnet.
I drink cold water and my throat is chilled.
A light goes on behind my neighbor's blinds.

I wonder if she, too, is godless. I wonder
what music brought her in from the ledge.

KAREN LITTLE

Along the river

He isn't a headline, or the viral video strap line:
contains uplifting scenes. They will never reunite,
the young man caught up in music, removing
his headphones to engage with the middle-aged woman
at the kerb. She was willing lorry-tonnes to flatten her.

He somehow read her mind, reminded her
of her son: another young man rare enough
to risk rebuttal, to ask someone if they were all right,
if they wanted to talk about it. So, she didn't roll
into the road, she walked home along the river.

SADIE MASKERY

No one can tell you

No one can tell you what you feel.
I can only say, this was the way
it took me, insidious,
contaminated each breath.
Emptiness is the wrong word.
I can't find them now, the right words
to explain the howl.
Nowhere left
but inward,
thoughts eating themselves
until all left was the solution
of not being, the simplicity.
Not to suffer not to be,
not to deal not to endure days
dissolved in dread of waking.
The mess stopped still. I wouldn't
be there. Except I was. And -
There was mess, there are places
I can't go now for the shame of it.

No one can tell you what you feel.
This is the way it takes me now.
Today, today, is real.

I get through today.
Tomorrow has options.
I don't have
to use them today;
get through today,
save for tomorrow,
keep in a pocket the power
that soon today will not be real,
only memory.
I won, made it all the way
to yesterday.
Every day of this life,
made it.
And today will be
last week
last month,
last year,
one day.

ANON

Suicide Roulette

I just want you to know, I know
Every time it starts, I see the signs, the twinkle in your eye
The devil may take me look makes me wanna cry
I wait with anxiety for it to pass in time
To know if the odds were with you this time?

Again and again
Over and over
Will this be the last time?
Was the last time I saw you
The last time I'll ever see you?
The loaded kiss goodbye?

Nights and days roll into one, long
Drawn out sesh laced with disregard and pain
Hurt of all kinds numb for you, but for your ones
Who love you No such release,
only more of the same pain drain

Babe I love you so dearly,
who is with you on your suicide watch?
While you dice with death so very nearly
Your spirit guide perhaps?
I hope for your sake he sees clearly

WENDY YOUNG

Don't judge

Until you've been spurned-

                     don't judge

Until you've been burned-

                     don't judge

Until you've been turned into less than human-

                     don't judge

Until you've been churned 'til you're sour as milk –

                     don't judge

Until you've been returned, turned out, turned up, turned down –

                     don't judge

Until you've been watched your life end before your eyes –

                     don't judge

Until you've stood on the edge of nothing –

                     don't judge

Until you've seen the future filmed,

previewed in the space of a day without you in it –

                     don't judge

Until you've walked empty bellied – full wombed –

                     don't judge

Until you've seen the spreader of the seed

left with you to deal with flaunting disloyalty –

don't judge

Until you've taken the last bus Sunday night embarrassed –
drained – walked up familiar streets that seem like no man's land –

don't judge

Until you've roared like a bairn flooding the gutter having no
one to run to –

don't judge

Until you've screamed and ranted and kicked and
created a scene in town like a raging harridan –

don't judge

Until you've implored – you've swung your fists –
you've made your situation clear and still been ignored –

don't judge

Until the five foot serene queen has looked at you
as an escapee from Storthes Hall –

don't judge

Until you've dragged your weary bones into the house –
head-butted the kitchen slab –

don't judge

Until you've decided that pills are the way out –

don't judge

Until you've swallowed and thrown up what you think is blood
'cause the capsules were just red and black – been back and forth
to the toilet to throw up –

don't judge

Until you've taken a mixture of what's on the shelf –
still empty bellied denying your 'self' whining in a haze
blinded in judgement –

don't judge

Until you've sat and tried to punch the problem out of your stomach –

> don't judge

Until you've been accused 'million dollar question –

is it mine?' by a cowardly thug –

> don't judge

Until you've bulged your eyes with alien drugs –

> don't judge

Until you've carried the regret not having 'suction' – '

cause the twat who put you in a position – begged you to keep it –

> don't judge

Until you're laid on a settee in front of a dying fire –

with your soul within it –

> don't judge

Until you've laid and sat – spewed up – wanted the end to begin –

> don't judge

Until you've met the Devil more times than a young girl should –

> don't judge

Until you've had: no plan; no hope; no support; not been the
underdog; kicked; slapped; punched; fucked without remorse –

> don't judge

Until you've had no idea what the hell is in front of you – see
only darkness–

> don't judge

Until you know the cost of abuse – money is invisible –

> don't judge

Until you've begged for a loan –

then a spitting mother who can't show hurt has thrown some
notes at you –

> don't judge

Until your cosy world is in tatters –

 don't judge

Until you've been told there's gold between your legs and that's all –

 don't judge

Until you're at the doors where the black hole beckons –

 your star's combusted –

 no prospect or expectation -

 you've stood in a road in Winter midnight –

 stars blurred by your tears with no fear of owt -

 your soul bruised and battered –

 you're nowt – chased dragons –

 fire flattened - you just ache –

 you have done with this existence –

 'til you've hung like a cocoon –

 'til you're a zombied mass of cells

 'til your brain is shattered –

 'til you're the Victim pulling that cord;

 taking the pills; firing the gun and

 SUICIDE IS ALL THAT MATTERS –

 don't judge.

MIKE GRAVES

Stairway

The stairwell is empty.
Squeeze through the narrow space.
Drop your bulky jacket on the floor.
Don't be afraid of the bite of the cold,
The bitter snake flowing into the cushion of warmth around you.
Put your fingers on the pane and push
You cannot save your childhood now,
Those stories of shame repeated at holiday dinners
Like eucharists to laughing relatives.
It is a Thomas a Kempis, clawing in the coffin of your
consciousness,
Crying out to crucify
both Christ and His Father.
Go on. Push.

SOPHIE CAMERON

I love you always

On Bideford bridge
The Council has lashed
Six foot metal railings
On top of the walls
To stop people from jumping.

She didn't want a funeral
She just wanted to disappear
Don't put my name in stone
She signed the note
Without a ripple.

But she wasn't there to stop them.

The funeral was not for her anyway
It was for her three daughters
Who carried that wicker coffin
Weighted down by the shot
That turned their mother inside out
And painted that headboard
With the bloody tears of nightmares.

It was for her friends
And for her family

To help them mark something
To begin to gather themselves up
To start building something
Over a black hole that will never be filled.

ALBY STOCKLEY

Grenade

You're angry with me today
You haven't said it
But you've given it a voice
You handed me a grenade
But you kept the safety pin
So I couldn't hand it back
Not when I was scared
You wouldn't put the pin back in

Pandora's box I discovered
Is never just one jar
There's a plethora hidden
In all our lives
But the one you gave me today
Was shaped like a biscuit tin
I went straight to my room and I hid it
An innocuous exterior
Belies the malignant content stock piled inside
I am fearful for the mindset
That gave action to the process
Of collecting what you now call your safety net

Previous resolutions

Gave sway to an action not yet carried through
Gave way to inaction and the Elephant we can't digest
Gives way to repeated internalised distress
Gives dependence on a content
That could disassemble all our lives one day
And I can't find it in myself to ever be angry at you
I know it's not an outcome
You'd want by choice to go through
There's a power that you play for
A tight rope made up of all the voices
That you fight against in different ways

You're angry at me
You haven't said it
But you asked me for something
I couldn't give back to you
Please forgive me, but I made two calls
Then drove the three hours back home
Listening to every group chat beep
Telling me you still had a heart beat

I am always humbled by the trust you give
The talks we have with truths laid bare
There's an openness and honesty we share
You told me once you were grateful that
I've never made you feel judged
Well my dearest that to me is what true friends are for
So when I said you're my family of choice
I meant it
When I said I except all of you
I meant it
When I said I'm here for you
I meant it

When I said no matter what
I meant it
You're angry at me
You haven't said it
But I've decoded you're recent messages
And there's a honey and a kiss left off your replies
But you handed me a grenade and
It burnt my hands when a I held it
So I drove it far from you
And thought of ways to diffuse it

You told me the next day
You'd made a new one
So I just messaged back
'I love you always' and I meant it

I wrote this after being handed a biscuit tin with 90 paracetamols and other tablets in, be-ing told simply "my doctor told me I have to give this to you" by my best friend. They then asked for it back when I was driving back home to Kent, 150 miles from where they live. I'd hid the tin in the boot of my car not knowing what to do with it.

KAREN CORINNE HERCEG

Down from the Ledge

Doubt is a whisper,
its very subtlety penetrates truth
with a seductive twist
weaving an insidious path through sureties,
unsettling certainty,
slicing ribbons of disruption in visions of hope,
a fragile thread that holds us
between now and the mystic.
Hell is where disbelief augments illusion
impairing our moments,
pinpoints of potential light restricted by will,
the lure of logic
disrupting our consonance with creation.
Our redemption is an interior voice
devoid of personality,
stripped down to the veracity of the cosmos.
In that step across the threshold
breath deepens
defying the lie of limitation,
sustained by a pilgrim of authenticity
boldly tearing at the numbness of its own presence
against the abysmal paralysis of the unrealized,
opposing the assassination of our worth.

EVE MCDOUGALL

TIK, TOK

My Blood is all over the place,
Horror and dread,
At the state of this creature's head,
He's so fucked up, got to be fed.

Feeding from violence of a psychopathic kind,
Doesn't care what he's done to my mind,
beastly madman a monster completely insane.

There is an almighty crash,
My body gets punched, kicked and severely smashed,
The size 10 boots into my guts so very harsh.

I get the razor blades,
Now I'm slain cut my arms to bits Just to get an ambulance away
from him.

No places left to go, or anyone left who wants to know.
Feel like dying all the time.

Raped, battered mortal shock of this body that can still function,
get back up and walk.

I won't be held down by this psychotic evil coward.
Staying brave fighting suicidal thoughts.

Beastly words running riot scrutinising me: "your worthless, stupid,
a nothing, you won't amount to anything".

The last straw was sitting in the asylum in a locked ward staring
at a TV
encased in a cage,

Somehow the will came flooding back something inside sparked
a light switched on,

I heard a radio playing Tina Turners song
"I will survive",

I hang on to the happy hopeful times,
hang on to the happy times.

Today has a tomorrow now,
Rising up from my own ashes,

I did not die grateful humble to be alive,
Rising up I did not die.

I hang on to the happy hopeful times,
I need not slay slayers for their time will come.

MEGAN GARRETT-JONES

Aladdin Trousers

When I was six, my Mum's friend gave me a gift
Her daughter was my play mate
Same age girls being convenient sleep over dates,
As was the occasion of this present;
A pair of hand sewn trousers
Handsome billowing beautifully patchworked
In the faraway style of Aladdin

Though Disney's version was on the big screen
These held more fantasy
With blocks of swirly patterns
Purple silks and turquoise satin
Each square a door to a scene in 1001 Nights
And a window to a time
In the life of the tailor.

Collector of magical patches
Designer of clothes that let the wearer
Be as much pickpocket in the bazaar
As princess in secluded garden,
Nomadic soothsayer, powerful magician.
Or curled up girl on the carpet
With a bowl of popcorn

That's really Turkish delight or a fruit she's never eaten.

My friend's house was so different to mine.
Two people instead of five.
A mum and daughter co-reliant
And this lady with a mysterious, majestic vibe.
I don't remember exactly, but when I was small
She seemed to be the type
To smoke long cigarettes and have a crystal ball,
And her daughter was naughty.

She took me to the cabinet of toiletries
A rainbow of lipsticks, when my mum only had one
That swum around in her oversized handbag.
There were potions and perfumes
And a whole new world of feminine hygiene
Just for fun we opened the wrapping on a tampon.

I lied and told them I only ate coco pops
When we stopped at the shops on the way over
And was rewarded with a sugary breakfast.
My indiscretion was discovered
But I got to keep the trousers and
I had the best time. Can I please go back next week?

The last time I saw Eleonora
At a Thai restaurant out for dinner
She was worn out by chemo and forlorn
Like inside she was screaming from boredom
Since her semblance of purpose,
A public servant's office,
Was denied because of her illness.
I never knew of her bouts of depression

Just had my impression that she was a big fish in the small
Dull pond that was Canberra.
She was the kind that would grant you a wish
If you were to set her free
Which was her only wish in the end
When she took that last step out a window.

I know I'm bringing you pathos here
But it's mixed with genuine fear
For the incredible women
Who can't find the nurture they need to survive
In our fucked-up vision of society.
Independent, private, talented
But wanting for like-minded spirits.
She had flair and magic to share
Once upon a time with children
When the window outside got sinister
I wish she had found a door.

MAT LLOYD

Blokes 2020

I started the evening
By telling him
That he looked a bit fat!
And he explained that,
"Well...
 every-time I bone your missus
she gives me a donut, slut!"
Cause that's how we were,
Him and me,
Him and us,
Friendly banter
And the odd
Over the top cuss.
Loads of bravado
But no false pretence,
And all of our jokes
At no one else's expense.

And that night,
We were trying to cheer him up
The only way we could,
With Jaeger bombs and tequila
Anything with alcohol was good.

Hell they'd done it for me,
With toasts of
"Screw her she's a tart"
And they were fully aware
Of my broken heart.
They never laughed at me
When I was acting stupid,
Or complained
When I was stressed,
They picked me up
And sat me down,
When I was a drunken
Mess.

But anyway, I digress...

Tonight
I had on my supportive hat.
I told him,
She looked like she apple bobbed
In chip fat,
And he laughed at that.
Cause that's how we were
Him and me,
Him and us,
Friendly banter
And the odd
Over the top cuss.
Loads of bravado
But no false pretence
And all of our jokes,
At no one else's expense.

Maybe, it's because we were blokes,
That we didn't show emotion,
But I'm sure that through the commotion
You can see that we cared.
My mate stared in to space,
Blank look on his face.
That's how I knew,
No amount of cheap shots
And bravado
Could change his mood.
Switch tactics say something crude!
Cause that's how we were,
Him and me,
Him and us,
Friendly banter
And the odd
Over the top cuss.
Loads of bravado
But no false pretence.
And all of our jokes
At no one else's expense.

That night my mate found salvation,
In whisky and pills.
His text saying "I'm sorry"
Still gives me the chills.
That last night a memory,
I remember with a blur,
Should I have said something different?
Nah, that's just how we were.

You know, I was angry at first,
What could I have said?

So he'd be breathing
And with me instead.
Maybe among the cheap shots
And bravadoon that day,
I should have said "I'd miss you dude!"

But he would have probably called me a "nob".

CAROL LYNN STEVENSON GRELLAS

A Daughter's Project / Getting over a Suicide

A daughter is supposed to be cherished,
saved like the white gardenia for fear
of bruising its delicate petals. She is tender

as the scent that travels behind her mother's
ear where all handpicked flowers should live.
But sometimes she arrives in her mama's suitcase,

leftover like the midnight sandwich on the bedside
table, postscript, or the moon's reflection on glass.
There's a reckoning that happens when a marriage

is over. A crass litany of things to share, the amicable
parting if everyone's graciously aware. But oh,
when a parent has died, there's an unfinished

debt for the nearly orphaned child. So, I crawled
inside my mother's baggage, unknowing
a space could be so dark. I cried when the latch

was untied, and a spark of light entered through
the keyhole mirrored in my mother's eyes.
Another day, she would say and primp

my pinafore with a sash of crinoline ties
But most lies are said in silence. I wear a family
heirloom; a golden locket around my neck,

my amulet filled with memories, cloudy dreams
of hope that people never really die. Even so,
I am the remnants of a father I used to know,

who momentarily forgot the scent of gardenias
behind my mother's ear and the handpicked
flower that lived there, so very long ago.

To the Year of Unknowing

In their perfect little house, fifty years
ago, with the dog asleep on his back,
under the coffee table, my mother
wearing her silk kimono, my father

with his bolo hanging around his neck,
half-eaten pancakes on dishes stacked
in the kitchen, the telephone's receiver
resting on its cradle in the hallway shelf,

the quiet of the morning not yet undone,
his duck decoys stashed in a bag before
his next big hunt, before the rest of life
took over, before he got sick before she

sent my brother and me to my room,
before she called the ambulance, before
I found him unawake before she read
his note, before there was a thing called

suicide hotline, or PTSD, or support groups
for vets after the war, before the moment
he decided life was unbearable, before
the eucalyptus tree beyond my window

looked like a monster through the sheer
of drapes, after the sun went down, after
my mother stopped caring about wearing
her pretty things, after my father's bolo

was just a souvenir kept in a leather
box, I open on days I can stand the memory
of what it felt like back then, before it
would be remembered as the before,

before I knew there would be an after.

CARRIE MAGNESS RADNA

People with Sad Eyes

They don't ever talk
about her last days,

but her 7-year-old grandson
heard the Emergency sirens
screaming outside—
as chaos
shook the household,
he hid in the attic
until it was quiet again.

The blood stains
never showed up
on the carpet;
the empty pill bottle
on the dresser
didn't gave others
any notice
at first—

Was she sad?
For a long time, yes.
 Why was she sad?

No one knew—

She was the artistic type:
always too sensitive.

She painted people with sad eyes.

Did they notice
her eyes were also sad?

Her grandson figured it out
forty years later
when he told his story
to his wife:
the chaos, the Emergency sirens,
him hiding in the attic—

a flash
of a covered body
floating downstairs
on a stretcher—
was it a dream?

He did somewhat remember
the days before she died:
so sad,
her eyes were empty of light.
She stared into nowhere—

No one knew
the gravitas of her pain.
What if they did?

Family Sorrows

Suicide has been
an activity carried
by the blood
of my father's family:

great-uncle & great-aunt:
both born with melancholy,
mixed with drinking & anger.
She expired first,
him 2 years later.

1st cousin:
he loved the wrong person.
Heart-broken,
he took a gun to his temple—

2nd cousin:
she attempted to kill herself
with a ceiling fan
when she was five.
At thirteen, she took pills.

Both ways failed.
She took her pain
& sang the blues,
& won a Grammy.

Other cousins
tried to numb
themselves
into oblivion,

the family pain is felt deeply
with roots planted
for thousands
of miles.

The ones who died
locked their
feelings away,
keeping silent

Silence = Death

I'm Miss Melancholy,
chasing the blues
like a Bengal tiger in heat,
since I was a girl.

At twelve,
I wanted to end it all,
to dull all my emotions
after the bullies
had abused me at school.

But then,
I heard God,
so I didn't.

Dad & Mom
tried to shield me
from the druggies
of my family,
but their/my inner pain
was real,

pulsing like blood
in a tree.

But now
my blues
are small
like kittens.

My armor,
once like
a rusted-up
Knight,
now wears
thin like a T-shirt.

I share my blues
in poems & songs
when I am down.

Suicide is the
last thing
on my mind.

MARTIN HEAD

What Could I Have Done?

At age fifteen my mate Billy nicked a
Suzuki Super Six and drove it into
A high brick wall. The copper said
There was no sign he even tried to brake:
I knew he was a mad kid, but
What could I have done?

Reggie, when huckelled by the cops'
Swallowed a whole hand full of acid tabs
Went into our local mental hospital
And when it closed he walked into the sea.
What could I have done?

While Sophie was at work her boyfriend hanged himself
From the staircase in her hallway:
He had tried before, in different ways
But what could she have done?

My mate David , while walking in the woods
Slung his own dog's lead over a bough and hanged himself
With his own dog's lead.
What could anyone have done?

And Sara, having put two kids through university
On her own, lay down in a warm bath and opened a vein.
What could they have done?
And when and if I've had enough of all this shit
Please remember
There is nothing that you could have done.

JASON WISTERIA

'A catch from above'

Not only friends
Very much like brothers
Mudlarks in the garden & the ditch
In faith & philosophy
Our similar paths
& wide expanses
We'd fill them with fun & laughter
Dreamy Days & chemical.
Adrenaline & chocolate.

Years after I'd missed you
I had this dream in colour
We had separated and gone our ways
You had headed for a hilltop tree on an outcrop
I had taken the goats path to the river.
Close by between ash trees and limes
I created a shack with bark & moss

Using tools I'd found in an abandoned house
It was here I found a dog tied up and rescued him
I hunted with Dom and snared our dinner
We danced among the rocks & roots by the river
Until we reached the sea

Here we found a sailing vessel with burgundy sails
We repaired the hull and set off towards anywhere
On a moonlit night I saw your smiling face in a cloud
A star in each eye
Across the seas we ploughed a furrow
Catching flying fish
& once ashore in a No Man's land
I met a mermaid tall & pure
A flagon in her hand
She washed my beard and made me fish cakes
Next day or so it seemed
It was a dream
On we swept towards who knew where
Dolphins, turtles, star fish said Hello
Then in a low blue haze one morning
Misty & turquoise & so fresh
We saw a bridge tantalisingly golden
Early birds screeched above us
On an instinct I dropped the net.
Deep & wide it splayed.
In the mists all went quiet.
I thought I heard a haunted voice ...
Seconds later an object hit the water above the net.
A catch from above I guessed
It was a baffling moment
Then in we hauled & struggled
The dog & I
Pulling & straining every sinew
Expecting tuna
Instead we found you
Battered bruised & breathless
Crying a big fat tear
With wet hair in your face

" I wanted another world
I cannot say why!"
We hugged & laughed
& Dom leapt with joy
To see us happy
Then reaching in my pocket
I offered you the oyster shell
The one I carried through thick and thin for you
From our time in Sandwich Bay
With 'Auntie Forbes'
In nineteen sixty-seven
When we were young and blonde.
Then after fish fingers and baked beans
And a tram ride on the hills
We set sail again
Time's winged chariot
Guiding us back but not in time
Not dwelling on the wake
Nothing was ever wasted
Not one single tear or smile
Not one single regret.
Then I knew
So much better
What love & friendship meant
& to embrace more often

JEREMY REED

Dead Number, for Matthew Lewis

Your daily quota soda juiced
with methadone before you'd call,
a drop behind reality
like a crash in money markets.
I go most days forgetting that you're dead,
your chocolate eyes a winning optimal,
the facial grammar of your black and whites
archived by the NPG
as frozen histories, like slicing time
into monochromatic salami -
John Balance, Francis Bacon, Saint Derek.
Today, apparitional fog paddles
round towers: an antler of magnolias
thrusts purple areolas into view.
What if you'd faked it - I mean suicide
in your Islington bunker, how'd I know
it happened as end-to-end completion
as part of the unedited future,
you gone into hiding on Romney Marsh?
I fidget with the question, you in mind,
in this translucent mass of orange fog,
eerily backlit, try your old number
still on my phone, like summoning the dead.

Do Ya

Remember the tiled maze of platform floor
at Warren Street underground, a boot-smeared
schematic of signposting
for a happening with unclear agency
the tube's apprehensive delay
with somebody about to jump

and restrained by an unnameable thought
or so you told me, liminially
your mother as a futures shape
without a body, but input

like psychic DNA.
You'd sort of half-turned, found me out
as though I'd understand
your oscillations at the edge
as total stranger, like we met

before this happened 3pm Friday
like the clean burn of foiled motivation
created something that you found in me
the tube arriving with a whoomph of shock,

me going back up to the street with you
to see you clear to the exit,
skinny drugged girl at a guess 23.

ANNE CASEY

She understood

That we are all one
    part blood & bone
    to two parts
broken star—

I never understood
    her in the moment,
    but hindsight is a sage
coach and efficient whip:

why she was late that day,
    how it might have sparked
    my adolescent ire, that
ever-stokable fire;

those long nights alone in the shop,
    bitter winter-dark solitude,
    my own aloneness
in the house behind;

how she would often seem
    to be only half-listening,
    lips moving out of time
with my words;

and the tension over books
　　　　never quite balancing;
　　　　the endless lists, in case
an intercession was missed;

how she knew pure compassion
　　　　runs to no human timeline,
　　　　how I missed that she had
dependents other than me;

how they leaned in to her
　　　　over that counter
　　　　year in, year out,
no matter the weather; how a kind

word or the promise of a novena
　　　　was enough for some,
　　　　under-the-counter
dealings for others—

a rushed parcel pressed into wringing
　　　　hands with a hushed *pay when you can*:
　　　　school shoes, a Communion
dress, community necessities

or Christmas niceties—
　　　　brightly wrapped in an
　　　　anonymous pile because
joy shouldn't stop at any threshold—

but it was her gift
　　　　of foresight that drove her
　　　　to lock the door that day,
that made her late for me:

racing down narrow muddy ruts
      to find him, rope-in-hand—
      his whole life lived in this
house with his own late mother.

Who knew, could have known
      how much she understood
      how we need less
than we believe;

how we can survive
      more than we realise;
      how we are all part
-broken;

how it was only as her blood
      & bone broke down, I understood
      how she had always been more
than two parts star.

AGNES MARTON

Time to Destination: Unknown

She's reaching out, no mask on,
to help me up.

By myself. If the bones
are strong enough to carry my weight.

She's hauling me upwards.
The light is piercing my eyes.
Throbbing, plunge.

Something sprained.

This stranger picks me up,
my arms around her neck.

Her shoulders smell like mum.
Huh, it's you.
I'm whispering, put me down.

She goes on, humming a tune,
chiding me, stop nagging.

SUZANNE FRENCH

There's always another day

There's always another day
Just wait till the sun comes up I say
it never fails to please or amaze

I know your soul is weary
worn out by pain, sadness, grief, madness
but just wait till the sun comes up I say
there's always another day

We're a long time dead
don't rush to that finish post in your head
you might miss something great
and my heart will break
if you make that mistake
there's always another day
Just wait till the sun comes up I say

Be kind to yourself
Be really, REALLY nice
you don't deserve this pain
treat yourself with the utmost love & respect
your life is a gift
Just wait till the sun comes up
Because there's always another day :))

PAT LEACOCK

AKA PDLpoet

Strength in Numbness

Where does the strength come from to pick yourself up?

When lethargy consumes you.
And even making a cup
of tea is too much!

And your skin is so tender to the touch.

Trips to and from hospital.
Key worker staff so hospitable.

Almost makes it bearable
to see them again.

But there's still the pain.
Burning like acid through your throat and every vein.

And the dreaded "C word"
has another name!

So what keeps you going?

Is it the fear of "THAT PILL"

Delivering life's final kiss?
Or the "ever after foreverness"
of the pleasures you will miss.

Such as the constant buzz from your phone.
Bombarded with favours
offered to you
By true friends and neighbours.

Reminding you they are there
For every step you take.
And you know what's so lovely...
None of their sentiments are contrived or fake.

Just their way of spreading love and good wishes.
As they happily bring gifts,
and wash up your dishes.

Sending fresh flowers.
Keen to talk of your hobbies.
And hope you realise that right now everybody's
Routing for you....
Thinking of you...
Here just for you.

With a warm cup of tea
And good company.

Giving you strength through the numbness.

You...me...WE!

MADELEINE F. WHITE

One for Sorrow...

One for Sorrow
Two for Fear
Three for Guilt
Four for Despair,
Five for what's Owed
Six for what's Lost,
Seven for the Silence
You've kept at All Costs.

As Darkness enfolds
The countdown goes on,
You can't breathe
You can't see –
Just grieve for what's gone.

YOU THINK YOU'RE ALONE.
BUT YOU'RE NOT.
SO, STOP.
DON'T FOLLOW THE STARKNESS
INTO THE DARKNESS.

Though life is a bitch
There is a Switch.

You just need to find it,
Put Power behind it.
Flick it, click it switch it.
The same as me, you'll come to see that:

If one is for sorrow
And two is for fear
And three for the loss of all you hold dear
Then four can be Light behind what is lost
Five, the People you tell of the cost
Six for the darkness Dispelled in this way
Seven for the Life beyond this today.

They'll be an eight and a nine
Atonement, Forgiving
And you'll see that Death is just Death
But Life is for LIVING.
And, Oh Boy, by the time you get to twenty,
And you realise you've gone from nothing to plenty –
You'll know without doubt;
That though life is still a bitch
You made the time to find that Switch.

And in this moment, right, now,
That choice is all there is.

HENRY MADD

Extraordinary Creatures

When I'm older,
and I've got a grandson or daughter,
we shall sit on a bench with a name written on it
and look at the world before us.
I'll tell them of a time when rivers
flowed through forests,
before landscapes were desecrated
to make space for cattle.

I'll them of extraordinary creatures,
Describe the magic of Rhinos or...Orangutans!
Like, "They were these, bad boy, ginger, mad things
that lived off ants and bananas
but then we bulldozed their home
and forgot about the planet."

I'll tell them of these creatures and so many more,
the ones that are gone,
that didn't make it through,
then, I'll pause for a moment...

and I'll tell them of you.

Of sunshine in a dark room.
Eco warrior.

How you called out plastic straws - before it was cool.

How your smile caused your cheeks
to bulge pregnant with laughter.
Radiating light like stars were born
in the pores of your skin
but, as their light grew,
so did the gaps in between
where darkness was hiding.

How the laughter in your cheeks miscarried
as that smile dropped
like ice caps crumbling into the ocean.

How you never stopped singing
while you suffered in silence, isolated,
seeking asylum from your mind getting blind drunk-
oceans like you could stop them rising.

I'll tell them ... How after 4 years
of not picking up the phone
we found each other
in a frozen home town beer garden on boxing day.
Dumbfounded and amazed we embraced
as if to say without you I fall apart,
and 4 years melted into seems like yesterday.

I'll tell them how that never really happened,
but, if I could see you again,
then that was always how I'd hope it be.

A friend told me energy doesn't die it only changes.
So, right now, you could be part of a tree
which I think you'd be happy about,
still caring for the planet.

I'll tell them how one day I'll join you.
And we will form a forest for rivers to flow through.
Before they cut us down to make memorial benches,
for grandsons and daughters to sit
and tell their grandsons and daughters
about

        extraordinary creatures,
            that they once knew.

PATRICK LYONS

Mirrors of the Dead

Broken skin on your chin,knees and shins
Get up done it again done it again
Jam jars wrapped around lamp posts-
cut free for all to see
legs backs, Heads
All the While watching,
watching mirrors of the dead,
mirrors of the dead

Broken promise only scam
Single window pain in broken frame
separate devastate isolate hearts that wait,
isolate hearts that wait
Fix the broken eggs she said,
I cooked them up, broke the hunger instead
Midnight fox is cleaning up ,
an rice is nice and ice cream has no bones
All the while watching mirrors of the dead,
watching mirrors of the dead,
mirrors of the dead.

RORY PADDLE
AKA RAWBYNATURE

It's Just the Face

My mental health is suffering
    I guess we both have that in common
perhaps we could be friends
    except my mind wanders off to deal with blows I try to soften
it often happens that way - I get angry
    at the unfairness in the world and
just sit there in a conditioned state of happy
    whilst mental health goes full vigilante
burying problems in their coffins
    locking skeletons in their closets
pulling elephants out of rooms
    upturning unruly prophets
so we can be king of the sofa
    rest our laurels smile and just slob it
drink the day poppet on play
    games mental health cannot pause for
and for sure I cannot stop it
    things for me are looking up but hang on
its suicide rates that ought to be dropping
    to their fate and not forgotten
I swear down my mental health contemplates
    hundreds and thousands of times a day
and that's not just a story topping

sure it's a bit of a morbid topic but I'm ok
I don't dissociate and I recognise the warnings of it
    I'm just not a fake no I ain't no Mary Poppins
but being honest when I create the picture I paint
    got Little House on the Prairie rocking
when I'm away with the fairies cotching
    it's fairly obvious I've escaped into a better
place where people are fair and forage
    give take and share the forest like a game of
kiss chase put to bed all troubles when they bare their foreheads
    but the torrents won't stop for mental health
it rudely awakens me from that little break
    I went on like a hurricanes hit the tropics
and suddenly all the small things stand out
    my eyes they strain their sockets and
as much as I refrain reframe restrain abolish
    let go of mental health so I can regain my fun and frolics
I guess it'll always be a part of me even if
    it's just the face of an ever ageing conscience

DAVID NO ONE

Wounded

Arterial spray siphoned through a crucifix
flooded with alcohol, Valium, & Ativan,
I write "sorry" on a page beneath fragments
of glass, no further elucidation necessary.
Cognisant of the emptiness of explanations
One word is enough (or too much?) no insight
can be gleaned from my tremulous scrawl
No matter how vainly I attempt to make it legible
My intent clots (the incision not as deep
as desired) the word morphs into a statement
of self reflective self, a scar unformed, a Momento Mori,
another blow on the on the bruise

SAM RAPP
(The Dyslexic Poet)

I Survived

My suicide started when I was 14
  unhappy in class as my writing was upside down
   another blow
    another fail
     another how lazy comment
      made me cry and wail

I ran from the school gates the railway track was near
  my fatal attack a voice called my name
   oi Sam where are you going
    that voice interrupted my plan
     back to class where the scolding finger
     demonised my spelling my grammar
     my being.

I'd survived an attack of mind
  I could see the sea and sand between toes and
   hear the horses snorts galloping mud in my face and
    seagulls racing playing games in the sky

Eight-teen tried again wrists arms cut marked with poor attempts

your spelling and grammar is way below your age
you won't pass exams or get a job
down and out washing pots like in Orwells London and Paris

I want to be a writer
what with writing like that you can't even read
without a finger moving the letters conjoined on a page
you can't do anything you don't know your times tables
I ground to a halt my mind was confused people
telling me how useless I am
why am I here

Years of counselling and pain
now a diagnosis is my gain
I survived my suicide I told it to go away
I'm dyslexic dyspraxic dyscalculia
I'm not stupid or useless
I'm a writer with a free sprit

My suicide never happened becauseI stopped myself falling deeper
into a tunnelled abyss of negative spirals
twists out of control
I wanted to live like birds and bumblebees
oceans rivers trees moving
and breathing our breath

I'm alive I'm dyslexic and proud
I survived

AGNES MEADOWS

Yellow

that driest yellow of life
in the hollow of the mouth

holds on in patches resisting
a death there in the midst of saliva

water vomit thick hospital dinners
and potassium dissolved in paper cups

all this to save the tattered body
all these days on the ward the yellowing

keeps up its watch at the back
of the mouth a bellow blooming me in

buttercups dandelions sunflowers
daffodils patient stains at the rise

of the tongue all this clinging
to life and life

clinging to me

GIL DE RAY

Erasing Awareness

The job was killing me,
12 relentless hours of it at a time.
The targets were superhuman
And my boss was a subhuman
Modern day slave master.
The radio and tv mourned
The collapse of the banks
And Gordon Brown mumbled
Apologies to racists
Opening the door to the hell
We would all soon have no escape from.
My record pressing business had been rendered no longer viable
By Pirate Bay and the digital revolution.
The CIA and MI6 were torturing people in Iraq and Afghanistan
As the Middle East descended into chaos.
Palestine was being bulldozed, pulverised and carpet bombed
By the untouchable forces of the IDF
I went on protest marches looking for an anger to match my own.
I found none.
Peaceful protest was a waste of time.
It achieved nothing

Waving placards at empty buildings.

Inside of me I felt that something

Was rotting

I was dying. Giving up.

I didn't have time to care.

I learned to hate everything.

The alarm clock, the stupid uniform I said I would never wear,

The flask of coffee I clung to, to get me through each cold, miserable morning.

The gods were laughing at me.

I'd taken a delivery job to get me past Christmas but they kept me on.

And to rub salt into my open wounds they placed me in the belly of

the beast.

Round and round I went,

Old Broad St, Threadneedle St, the banks, the fucking banks.

The Worshipful Cunts of Guildhall.

The absolute pits of humanity.

The truth was there was no crisis in the City.

It was booming

Champagne for breakfast.

Champagne for lunch.

Cocaine for dinner.

Big belly laughs easing

Quantatively

I wished I could broadcast a live stream to the rest of the country

Choking on austerity.

Everything was a lie.

Everywhere people were trying to raise awareness of this cause and that.

I wanted to erase my own.

I knew too much

I longed for the end.

It ground me down.

In my mobile cell I watched helplessly as the police killed Ian Tomlinson

On Threadneedle St.

I saw it. Felt the anger.

An impotent rage.

I carried it around with me

Unleashing it on unsuspecting members of the public.

I started to fantasise about blowing up the Bank of England.

I was there every day

With my trolley packed with deliveries from Fortnum and Mason.

I imagined they were packed with explosives.

Martyred,

A future icon for anarchists and jihadists.

One night on the drive back to the depot in Camden

I pulled over on Grays Inn Rd, snow cascading against the windscreen.

I killed the engine and cried uncontrollably:

It had finally come to this

I knew I had to end it somehow.

The next day the doctor tried to put me on Citalopram, that's what they do.

The National Health Service had become a street corner pusher for big pharma,

Pills for any ills.

In Afghanistan the opium fields were being harvested by the CIA

And America's great opioid crisis was no longer a pipe dream,

I sat waiting at the clinic for the therapy I'd had to fight to get.

"Are you mental too?"

Said the guy sat opposite

"I guess so"

I replied weakly.

In the therapist's room I opened my wounds.

A lifetime of shit you had no idea you were carrying around with you.

Heartbreaks, misunderstandings, lies and denials.

Bad choices, death and stupid reprisals.

All of it, went in the bin

Along with the shattered ego.

Trudging around Hyde park in the snow with a friend

I had the persistent feeling that I could never go home again.

"If you're not depressed there's something wrong with you" I told
him.

And he laughed knowing I was probably right.

If you want to change anything then you have to start with yourself,
my therapist told me.

And I believed it.

I unravelled in front of my friends and my family

It wasn't pretty

But it was necessary

For me at least.

The road back had been destroyed, mainly by myself

Sabotaged and booby-trapped.

Like the slowly withdrawing forces of the American and British war
machine post shock and awe.

The memories never leave.

So I imagined new roads,

Roads without restrictions or traffic.

Roads that weren't even roads,

I ran into Dead ends and cul de sacs.

Coming out even more determined than ever to find the right path forward.

It still eluded me like it had previously

But I kept going

Alone.

Half alive.

In time I exorcised the ghosts of my past and found

New experiences.

New friends.

New ways of dealing with the crushing

Inhumanity that rules the minds of those with power to enforce it.

This is where we are.

Full of intentions,

Good and bad.

Searching for a peace of mind

That has eluded us to this point in time.

SIMON MILES

On Chelsea Bridge

Looped like medals to bygone courage
lights pause along the edge of Chelsea Bridge
after dark and then hurl their gold into the deep
Treasures - bright and precious - which keep
the Thames alive with flames of cherished light
that rescue this river from drowning tonight

DAVID ERDOS

Let's play these words as Ace

It is there in Jacques Brel, as glamourised by Scott Walker: The song 'My Death,' like an anthem on the unsteady air Broadcasts in. It is a strange but soothing sound, safely Housed by Scott's midnight Angel, as opposed to Brel's Own sweat and frenzy, which made the idea of life itself Echo sin. I have heard this piece of music all year Without having to resort to the stylus. Now, as we face A new needle, its resonance plays, stark but true. As Engel And Brel's ghost duet sees them transposed into a key Beyond voices. Unless of course, dogs can hear it, Or perhaps the morning birds in review. The art Of wrapping peoples' pain in a song is both cure And sickness; if we can express and recover And encapsulate, then why drown in a dry and featureless Room, removed from the real we once treasured, And clawing the walls to risk ruin and cause the house Of the self to fall down. All of my life I have felt that all Problems and binds can be traced in some way, back To others; you can inherit conditions, genetic faults And world views, leaving no space for the self to find Its form and to flourish. Already at birth, death seems Written as you spend each day charting its oncoming path Clue by clue. And yet, happiness blooms when you chance To fill your time with distraction. These private poses, Ifwell crafted enough, spark careers; as if every flower Were flame, bidden through earth, ripe and rising; Ours to both smell and savour, as if one could decorate Each thorned fear. Until of course, you are pricked. Then the blood will cry through confusion. For tears Can bring bleeding. Ejaculation, saliva and micturation, too, Each has pulse. That such panic can stop in arythmic arrest And conjecture. Which I embroider at night, locked and lonely As I find myself, in and as, a fat Hamlet, talking to the long Sought dead through my skull. I live in my late Mother's house, Where photographs frame her spent body. I also know that Everything I own will survive me, even these pens and books, And Cds. Often, so much has scant worth as even the glow Of the ghost does not reach me, despite the fact I search for it, Dusting down spells and shadows, and wishing that she was Here with me, or, I was with her and my dear dead Dad, hourly. They wrench away at us, the gone, as we bustle and throng At Dream's station. For, grief, like the train, provides ticket To a further coast and glazed day that we are unable to see Even if it feels so familiar. The dead incite and invite us along This secret path, this ghost way. We can just get on board And pay no heed to the schedule: a flick of the wrist, a fat Swallow and my family reunite. I haven't been properly Touched in a year. Will the next be one self inflicted? Instead of masturbation's parody of affection, will a razor Rip death's love bite? I measure this motion each day As I wait to work and recover. As my bank unbalance starts Bleeding will the house's held language soon translate Into tomb? They will have to bury me with my books, In a pyramid Bungalow here in Uxbridge. A failing pharaoh, Once golden but rusted and run down all too soon. Or, rather out run by events, as survival becomes Science Fiction. The former futures imagined were never as terrifying As this. Now fate and fear feel mundane as things appear All too distant and suicide's sidestep avoids the jackboots Of Judas and co., come to kiss. And yet, yesterday, Myneighbour rang to ask me a favour. Her husband has cancer, And they were at UCL for his tests. The Doctors needed The brand of his recent Antibiotic. My neighbour having thrown The carton away called and asked me to search through her bins. I said yes. They needed the name of the pills and she couldn't Remember. I located the

Nitrofurantoin and happily, this allowed The process. I had done some good in a day and after a year Without, I felt purpose. It didn't feel like my mother, the woman I used to love, or my friends. But it was both a ghost and a gain And the Jacque Brel song dipped in volume. I have the empty Packet here as I'm writing. It is a totem of things still untasted As the tiny useless box seals all ends. It has quickly become Its own room that will at the very least represent me. Even in the dark its shape serves me as I try not to douse My own light through fear's stealth. I have done a lot of things In my time, but alone, the gain is hard to grasp, I'll be honest. And I am neither brave, or, a coward, or have enough of each To yet wreak that sort of revenge on myself. I would leave No-one behind. I am vital to none. Friends will miss me. And yet, in that loss; liberation. I should open a deck of cards. But cards bore me. Let's plays these words as Ace.

DAVE MANKIND

Let's All Hang Together

Let's all hang together
Let's all hang together

Just for a little while
You know it won't be forever
Safe to say sometimes it may feel that way

Let's all hang together
Let's all hang together

Because time flies even when you're not having fun
This journey lasts an eternity
And you've only just begun my son

Let's all hang together
Let's all hang together

Kicking and screaming into that good night we slide in
Way out on the horizon
Well everyone has to die somewhere

Let's all hang together
Let's all hang together

We can watch them relaxing in the ruins of civilizations nadir
There's nothing to fear here
For without love there is no death

GILL FEWINS

The Day After I Kill Myself

The day after I kill myself,
Birds will still sing.
People still shop,
Children play.

The day after I kill myself,
The pain will stop.
For me at least,
Other's scream.

The day after I kill myself,
I will not know.
I cannot tell,
I have ceased.

Will the sun still be shining bright?
From a blue sky?
Will stars glow in
Inky silk?

I will not see the sun again,
I will not feel
Rain on my face.
Goodbye world.

Perhaps, perhaps, perhaps I'll stay.
Just one more night
Just one more day..

KIRSTY ALLISON

Install the Update

I wasn't suicidal
I just had a death wish
           Self-destructing firework, reflecting in the gutter.

Chasing Hemingway, Grace Jones, Warhol
             Bukowski, Bowie, Bacon
      into the bars that they made famous,
      serving Talent Gateway cocktails.

Walking Physic Gardens, smoking in the herb aisles with spirit ghosts,
My skin absorbing Everything.
          Writing my own religion, away from religious wars.
            Waiting for the midnight cab, with my bin bags.
Trying to recover from what had entered.
          The first breakdown after being spiked with PCP at college,
after a rape at 14, which I dealt with by getting embedded in the
embers of Hawkwind.
          They gave me pills to manage that,
          Which seems a bit mental now

      So I stayed up all night for weeks
searching for the solstice party,
             Pounding Wicklow and Dublin, living
           walking, skipping, picking wild mint
    Carried into generic mass experience,
    the labyrinth, singing Duran Duran

I felt lucky not to come out being called Schizophrenic.
I wasn't, but the doctor fresh out of a Gap year in Thailand, wearing necklaces like he's some kinda new age feminist but he's just a young sawbrain quack,
my Mum thinks.

    Face like he's working behind an expensive deli on
    minimum wage, thinking you should buy a bigger slice,
    because he would, if he was you.

We all do it, in the Neo-liberal haze of judgements with few facts.

    Dosed on Largactyl and pre-historic shellshock drugs
I'm here in the club of Manic Depression.
  Closer to Jimi Hendrix, Virginia Woolfe and Blake
   Inveterate heroes legitimised in Madness.

    Fired from a career I'd died for, after being wiped and rebooted once already.
    Blanked again.
Zero:
An unused AirBnB with a never played guitar and an unworshipped Buddha.
I couldn't afford that though, I couldn't afford shit.
I'd never be able to
 My inability to pull the duvet high enough to hide beneath.
    Maybe that was their treatment, to make me hate myself so much.

    We never spoke of mental health
    It was always illness
    in the factory which owns the drug and the cure
    Every pill, consuming Dysfunction

    Admitting to stress is half the problem.
    Better to keep a stiff upper lip and barge on through.
    Believing that actually, everything is okay
    They do it. So better to be like Them.

Eventually I got up.

In the library, I rifled through Everything
Prozac Nation was the thing that came closest
But I took the lithium for two years
Copywriting about beige jumpers

I began to help others.
Zine workshops. Teaching. They called me a professor, in the end.

Now I know Labels are for Others.
And They don't have to last

Women are used to smiling whilst being fucked

Did I ever say I was crazy?
Did I say was Mad?
"I was the maddest in the mad unit," said the head nurse.
The craziest she'd ever seen.

That fades.
Out of mind
In Meditation
Like fireworks
That go too far
Like he, me, and the doctors

Not everyone loses their driving license every so often. Or their
bank card PINs.
I cannot hold on to myself.
My depression ebbs like some image I'm supposed to be scared
of - the kids about to nick your phone.

Now it would all be different.

.

JUDITH MOK

The Whetter of the Knife

No shame would ever redden his days.
He could have shown the eager, entirely,
how much he enjoyed his circus and its tricks.
He should have made spectators pay to watch the things he did to me,
turning me into this acrobat of pain.
But he preferred to keep me in a bulwark for his silence,
this pschyco's place where he tortured me.
This is how we do things in my country,
he said, a proud and fervent nationalist,
causing distress of a broader spectrum ,
seen through the narrow end of his binoculors,
It made me suffer the cutting shards of a kaleidoscopic feast.

And then, a horrid kiss. Not so ,on my lips.
With it, he burned the earth under my feet,
the songs in my soul, *the touch of real.*

Where it soaked the ground I wished for his blood to feed my gardens,
their putrid stench through my opened windows and music,
camelias, gardenias a tango tune, ragged.
And still: I loved.
I loved his screaming wounds, his sunken sores licked with my
pickled tongue.
Help me.

DAVID AXELROD

Nothing Monumental

Granite gravestones,
weathered two hundred
fifty years, barely boast
their famous names.
Smaller, gray slate
headstones have lost
their characters, simply
marking bones below.
Nothing monumental
for me, nor should
there be. Ozymandias,
Ramesses, Shelley, recorded
in history. Me? Lately,
I observe scenes and
picture myself missing.

BILL WOLAK

Lost in Darkness

Look at how
all fleeting things
end up lingering
in the dark earth.

There, the touch
of water transforms
the tiniest seeds waiting
among the shadows.

A secret openness gathers
preparing to welcome
some unknown,
unimaginable light.

If you're alone all night,
if solitude becomes unbearable,
dream like those hidden seeds
lost in darkness.

Who knows what
might reach out for light?
Who knows what delight

might unfold?
Uncertainty is never
a disadvantage.
It's the unrivaled opportunity
to welcome the inconceivable.

JAMES RAGAN

To a Mother and Child at the LA Mission Shelter

I, too, in the death-wick of the Kennedy days
drifted blindly through the innocent loss.
I, once trembling through the fires of a *Tien An Men* lamp,
wept my pillows into mirrors of glass.
I saw each day in the Darfur camps the eyes of an infant
shutter black, and with my thoughts fractured
by their abstract glance, I still did not know
the ache, to hope for nothing at all.
And out of the mind's compassion
have I taken the path to forgiven history
to know what hemispheres of the heart
you've had to cross. What cicatrix of a world-wound
a single word might heal, remembering
how frayed the ill-knit bond
between your vision and your will,
remembering how high from the world's mind you'd fallen,
on whose broad shoulder you now climb
to wail your words of forgiveness to the continents beyond.

CATHERINE ALICE WOODS

Rocket Ships and Fireworks

Curly hair, kindest eyes,
When I think of you my heart grows three times in size.
You are special, unique, one of a kind
But sometimes you are distracted by the troubles in your mind.

Yet you need not worry
I have a cunning plan
We take those little troubles
One by one in hand

We put them in a rocket ship and send them into space;
Our backup plan is fireworks, we light hundreds just in case.
Then it's time to settle down, on the night's ground we lay.

And watch them one by one, shimmer and fall away.

Now all is quiet, all is still
But the sound of your breath, your lungs it fills,
There is such beauty in this sound.

Let it stay there forever... with the hope we have found

FERN ANGEL BEATTIE

Mining Rubies

With white knuckles I cling to the edge
of my mattress and sanity, remembering
another night like this ten years ago,
laying on the opposite side of the same bed
and fantasising about the lick of the blade
mining rubies on the underside of my forearm.
I couldn't help but imagine how the cuts would look
like miniatures of the glass rocks that used to rest
on my great-grandmothers' electric heater,
another ten years before that.
Their translucent jewels warming my face
after an afternoon playing in her garden, safe
in the knowledge my whole family would live long,
happy, healthy lives because I'd thrown a penny
down her wishing well that morning to make it so.
Then knowing I should probably uphold my end
of the bargain I place the knife down flat
as a sorry heart monitor beneath my duvet,
sleep with it like a defensive weapon instead.
No matter how many times I arrive here
it is love that always save me, each summoning
hotter and more searing than the last.

AMAR AAKASH

Messiah Puppy

A mission impossible for me to carry out ,
this act of self-immolation.
In the dark tunnels of tumult,
I fought day and night.
Like a failed prophet,
I sermonized on the subject.
But in the end, *Dharampadda, Holy Bible,* or *Bhagwat Gita*
they all amounted to nothing,
and crumbled into a wasted mound of sawdust
to become a two-month-old spotted puppy.

To begin with, Mom started showering complaints,
to shame me. I couldn't choose a profession,
couldn't find a way to earn a living.
Then my girlfriend changed colors
and finally distanced herself.
I saw no income coming my way
in weeks and months.
Some admonished me to save me:
Life isn't just an effort to eke out a living,
nor is the ability to feed your self
thrice a day a triumph.
Acquiring a roof over your head,
not the ultimate accomplishment.
You think it's feasible for everyone
on this earth to reach the top and become wealthy?
None had proper answers.

Why were people with or without degrees jobless?
Isn't it old-fashioned to name a poor man a thief
or label someone ugly a witch?
But to lose a second lover at 39
was more horrific than being
without a food grain in my stomach for days.
Life's boundaries always slither
across borders of meal and shelter.
There were these disheartened human being
who died out of million failures in life,
and there were others, neck-deep
in debt ready to give up the ghost.
I'd known some who hung themselves
for being jilted by the loved ones.
Yet there were others who opted
to swallow angry pills to seal the final exit.
Many a times, I've laughed at their
dead bodies arriving at the cremation ghats.
No matter what, the lightning strikes on all,
regardless of time or place.
But that a two-month-old spotted puppy
could save someone's life I'd never heard.
In one of the blind alleys of Kathmandu
before getting waterlogged
into the bottomless bog land of despair
as I lifted my poisoned cup
I'd no idea that a soft soggy tongue
of a puppy licking the bridge
of my foot could have brought
me back to the flaming fields of life.

Translated from the Nepali by Yuyutsu Sharma

TIM KAHL

The Fermata

Everyone has something to blame their parents for,
an overly doting mother, a father too stern,
a general lack of concern as the parents grow
into their lives. They take a child with them so that
there is a witness to their shortcomings. The flaws
embed once they are seen, and then the child,
spiraling into adulthood, has pockets filled with them.
Add to this a growing list of regrets.
The choices made reverberate within the walls
of the chest. They drive by with their threats,
or they simply annoy like a jingle for a despised product,
one that has earned your contempt for being so pointless.
Yes, that's you, trapped in a cage of bad genetics
and bad decisions. Let's say you're feeling thrown away
or someone you trusted has left. Perhaps you were
shunned or publicly shamed—whatever the case,
despair has driven itself deep like a railroad spike.
Is this the end note, held with fermata until
the conductor's hand signals stop? The note lingers
in the air, poised for closure, but its resolution
doesn't come. The note hangs on and on in open space
and seems ridiculously long. It's perfectly absurd.
Days and weeks pass. Muffled sounds from the back
of the theater drop into the mix. So do the sounds of
street trafficand the thrum of escaping trains.
Another year is gone,and you are laughing madly,
laughing at the gurgle of your own turning stomach.

GERARD BEIRNE

Ways of Survival

Forehead to the night
Silver moon of steel

Tongue to the air
Vials of beaded shell

Neck to the shore
Braided waves of hemp

Throat to the light
Filament and wire

Wrist to the horizon
Blade of sea and sky

Stomach to the birds
Shrieks of sharpened beaks

Body to the water
Sinking stones of air

Dusk to the dawn
Hope from despair

TIMOTHY GAGER

Deathiversary: Years and A Day Late

Thirty years later
the death of a friend, still,
bleeding out, still, angry
I no longer really remember
the exact year (31 years or 29?)
I can't calculate…I've forgotten how—
I have forgotten a lot

I don't know where
his family is now
parents, a sister, his brothers
Steven and ….
Tom, that's his name… ,
lives here somewhere
in Massachusetts I can't remember

the town like many old memories
good or bad get shuffled around in my head,
yesterday…was the day,
yesterday, was just a Wednesday
yesterday, a day where I could feel the knife
jousting my wrist the way his did,
within all these thoughts that are not actions.

SANDRA YANNONE

Grief

One year later Harry Nilsson is dead
at 52. I'm standing outside in the dark
watching a sliver of my neighbor
through an errant blind. His left hand is a fist
which rests against the right. My grief is this watch
with the hand that sticks near the two
like the stiff backhand of the man
which stops just short of the woman's face
for too many years.
                    It is for the mother
whose son believes his blood is always blue
no matter how many times he's seen
the results of his own cuts. His wrist retains
its own vanity; the bones keep
their anatomical distance
under the skin.
                    It is for me in the restaurant
as you clamp a bracelet to my wrist
while looking straight into the woman's stare
from across the room. She sees nothing
she needs to see. I am her substitute.
Your name is the name she wants
wrapped to her wrist. At the other tables

men are paired off, bending toward each other
in the guise of eating soup. Each gives his tie
an occasional yank to keep away
from our business. They don't intervene.
They are no better than you.
                   It is for my finger,
the recipient of a cut while opening a bill.
Failed Visit: Mental Heath. A five-dollar charge.
I suck for the blood, check my watch
on the other wrist. Harry Nilsson's still dead
only longer.

YOGESH PATEL

Hofstadter's Strange Loop

Rapids you're in are only calm
Waters up and down streams
All roads go stray
Unless you know the destination
A scarecrow keeps the birds

Out instead   can watch the stars

ANNA HALBERSTADT

A Warm Weekend In May

First warm weekend in May,
a single puffy cloud like foam in a cappuccino
on a perfectly blue background.
At Union Square, behind
bouquets of lilacs in buckets
with cold water,
an eight-year-old future math prodigy
is playing a blitz with a middle-aged
chess professional
of narrowly local ranking,
a dollar fifty per game,
at a folding table,
proud father watching behind his son's back.
After a hard week at work,
feeling almost let down, without a purpose
other than boring house chores,
drained for once in a long time
by people.
Longing for respite from the crowd:
parade of dancers in pink tutus,
pirates in feathered hats,
passersby greedily
absorbing sun rays

after a long stretch of cold and gloom.
Thinking of a woman in *Ida* filmed jumping
out the open window to Bach's
"Concerto for Two Violins"
beautifully,
like an Olympic diving champion
or a tired angel descending back
to heaven away from people
who still wouldn't get it together.

MEGHA SOOD

The Note

Walking on the ledge
between the thin boundary of
living and the dead
I want to break the illusion
of being alive anymore

Just a step more
A little shove
and a push,
will break the long slumber
the nightmare
the facade;
I have been draping
at the core

That constant irk
that feeling of
being lost in the crowd
the deep soliloquy of the soul;
unheard and bounced back
every single time
leaves me frozen
numb to the core

Counting my failure
as the slashes on my wrist
and fighting
hard to fill the emptiness
with the broken pieces
of a puzzle left undone
forming a picture of gore

Here I am walking at the ledge
on the brink of life
and death
carving those fallen memories
on the bits of the paper
as my goodbye note.

PATRICIA CARRAGON

Just Say I Love Him
(sung by Nina Simone)

his engraved name on stone
tells me he's not coming back

the mistakes made
the regrets that haunt

dreams can't revive what's lost
rain comforts my face & hands

trees stripped of youth
wait for me to pass

a wilted red rose
finds perpetual sleep

grief is laid
to rest

DARIUSZ TOMASZ LEBIODA

The Last Letter Of Romek Jaskier
(With permission from his parents)

Dear mother and you, father,
forgive me for what I'm going to do
but I've no more strength to struggle with myself
It's all so strange – a similar day to the day
like two drops of water –
I would like to go back to the times
we used to visit Grandma together
and swim in the pond and fish all day long.
But everything seems hidden now somewhere,
far away as if I'm a noboby, unwanted
to someone behind the frosted glass.
Don't think it's only about my girl, Halinka –
I can't explain it more precisely
and I know it would always be like this

Please give my room to my brother
and give him a hug from me, also give him
my jeans shirts and my Moped too

I bid you farewell!
These are my last words.

P.S. Please convey my love to everybody

Translated from the Polish by the poet

AMANDA GOVAN

Life Drawing

"Samaritans, can I help you?"
I know nothing, have nothing of you.
Not even a name.
All I hear is "That'll be five pounds fifty love".
Your final face to face - paying the taxi fare.
A noisy silence. I hear you stumble on stairs.
Breathing uneven. Emotional pain.

"Take your time, do you want to talk?".
Down the line I was there.
Mine the privilege of your final plea:
Blurred, slurred words I barely heard.
 "Don't go, please stay....." Fading away.
No cry for help.
I don't know why you made this choice.

I cradle the phone to my ear,
"As long as you need me, I'm here."
Hoping that in your lonely reaching for a caring voice,
as you return the gift,
you find your place
and the peace denied you in life.
Your final release closes the call.

Closes my shift.
Later, as I draw black, dark-smudged lines.
Mulberry, indigo, navy and ash.
I hear again your breaking words.
Feel your broken mind.
I don't understand. I only draw mankind.
You drew broken breaths.
I'm drawing life, you drew death -
I'll never know why.
But I'llcherish the honour of that last goodbye.

JOHN PRASTITIS

Light Pours Out

"Samaritans,
Light pours out
Blacker Bluer
Chromatic shift
From that to this
Staring back at a weaponised sea
Haiku
Seppuku
I love you
Pharmaceutical negredo albino
Cast a spell for snow
Holy cow
Hellenic crow
Just to dam the river!
S flow
A sinister funk in pastel colours
Tsars in tar and rats to stars
Stare at ceilings plywood coffins
A buffet hymns the mourners limbs
I think of them

LUKE SULLIVAN

I Stand on the Quay

I stand on the quay
The darkness around me
Wind breaking my back
And the waves cascading me in

I scream

My cries fall silent drowned out by the gale
It's difficult to inhale
My mind writhes with the pain
I face into the storm and wait to fall in

I could go in

Take that final step and fall
Allow the sea to consume me
beaten and Ripped into the rocks
Through gritted teeth I smile at the thought

But they'll miss me

My safety my unit with one so new
Imagine what could happen to them without me

But it's cold
And I'm wet and all alone
So I think I'll just.....

Go home

When I get there she's packed
Crying she has to go
My world leaving through the door I just dragged myself in so.

Fuck no....

You moaned at me that you didn't wanna be here
And I very nearly wasn't here
But I came back to you
So damn you woman with your bicycles and buttons
It's not open for discussion

YUYUTSU SHARMA

You see it coming, Lincoln Centre

The studio of ashes,
an array of soot colored pillars,
a line of homeless urine
deflating the glory of a jazz city
bought once with
some stray patches of clouds,
and a streak of Avalokiteshvara's
thunder smile...
A fear you fear to fear,
a stench of a body
on the edge of Fifth Avenue.
'I need to come back,
I need a chance to make
an honest living' placard
placed atop an empty paint
bucket turned upside down
in front of the squatter busy
reading a used copy of Power Games
on a neat pavement outside
Starbucks Coffee, a board

of trinkets for sale behind him,
his brown German Shepherd
with its healthy coat hanging out
with him like a cool buddy
and the spacious street's silence
being punctured intermittently
by the screaming ambulance
cries of a million hyenas...

Outside Lincoln Centre
beneath entertainment billboards
you step down the subway stairs...
The train comes hurling at you.
You see it coming, 1,2 or 3,
an anger boiling
from a betrayal in your brain,
and with all your might
you want to leap across the tracks
and crash into it
and, perhaps,
end that whole Woolf story.
Then it slows down,
and comes to a halt,
and engulfs you and your wrath
into its big warm belly...

CARLOTTA ALLUM

We Watched Her

Hannah was always striking, angelic long hair,
Hannah stayed with us a lot, roaming the house
dressed only in an oversized Stone-Roses tee shirt
    We watched her

Hannah could write beautifully, cursive, neat beyond her years
Hannah liked to dance, as a child on the stage in the West End,
the Royal Ballet School took note
    We watched her

Hannah was super smart, reading Natural Sciences at Cambridge
Hannah was sent home in her first term
after setting fire to herself in front of her tutors on stage
    We watched her

Hannah spent hours in the shower and washing her hands
Hannah was weighing everything she ate
She was painfully thin
    We watched her

Hannah was working as a dominatrix
Hannah had lined the walls of her room with tin foil

as people were listening
        We watched her

My psychiatrist asked me
if there was any mental illness in the family
I think of Hannah, her light burning bright
When Hannah was well, she embraced life, she danced
        I admired her, watched her

Hannah was on a suicide ward outsmarting the nurses
Hannah kept back medication and smuggled in a plastic bag
Her mum knew, "She's going to do it"

"PLEASE, WATCH HER"

        They didn't watch her

From the Press:
As a result of her death, Cambridgeshire and Peterborough NHS
Foundation Trust made changes to their patient observation policy.
It would only have taken around eight minutes for Miss Allum to
take her own life.
"For us, reliving our worst fears that Hannah might take her life
and our endless efforts to make those caring for her recognise those
concerns, has been, at times, impossible to bear. We will al-ways
feel that Hannah was failed by the trust. We understand that certain
things are now different as a direct result of Hannah's death, but this
is too little too late for our dear Hannah or for us. We want Hannah
to be remembered for her beauty, intelligence and wit."

DEAN STALHAM

Daddy Duties

Let me tell you this right from the start
The words you are about to hear and read
Come directly from my head
Shooting at you from my heart
Letting you know first
Before any of you doubters out there
Get the thirst
For idle and useless gossip
Lies that can make you trip
Over your own big fat lip
That will follow you forever
Like a curse
Suicide
Is by no means
A fair ground ride
I knew a guy
Pretty damn fly
Was tall flew high
A toothy smile
As wide as a mile
Not being weird
He wore a great – great beard
And is the case

His tattoos
Were as well fucking ace
You'd think a guy like that, a handsome guy like that
Top hat – top cat
Would have everything to live for?
But not by this sods law
Life is never perfect
Life often comes undone
Underlying sadness, madness
Devoid of endless fun
Happiness you strive for
Happiness you're alive for
Happiness deserved by every daughter and every son
A son any mother would die for
A mother who maybe should have given a hell of lot more?
Not ever - ever closed the door
Paul Butters
Was not a nutter
He was a boy with mental health issues
That made him and those closest to him
Reach out for the soft boxed tissues
He was a boy with a mental health disease
One that made this boy
Very- very ill at ease
It strickened him- weakened him
By no means a tease
Refused to give him release
Mental health
That he often had to deal was forced to deal Alone –
With no one but himself
Doctors gave him medication
That gave him unification
Self -surveillance

Like a high wire walker
With a false sense of balance
A bed without a valance
Mental health disease
So cruel – so callous
Then out of the blue one day
The doctors in their infinite wisdom
Decided it was time to take this crutch of medication away
Almost on an evil whim
Not realising how it devastated him
He shouted and screamed WHY!
Don't you know?
Inside he'd cry
I could – now – die
For three nights he came into my room
Head full of promise
Zoom zoom zoom
Plans to make an al – boom
In his room
Honest music
No need to trend
Making sweet sweet songs
With his ex – girl friend
Who could sing without a fail
Like the sweetest nightingale
Near or far
He was at her side with his loyal guitar

Those three nights
I saw and witnessed a man
Who had the most positive – plan
No Desperate Dan
A man not afraid to show his hand

A man ordering American burgers
And thick vanilla milk shakes
A man that seemed to me
Was about to make the earth quake
Ordering microphones and speakers
Smiling like a pleasure seeker
Signing with the man
Sent from Amazan
Please don't correct me for saying it wrong
I know it's amazon
So what then happened?
Became distorted
Mis shapened
Contorted
Un reported
I went away on daddy duties
To look after my babies
My daughter's - my beauties
I came back after five days
Not the longest time to be away
Had no reason to think everything
Was not okay
Not au fait
A shift in time delay
As soon as I opened the front door
I knew something wasn't right
The unmistakable death smell
Had wafted through on a tainted day and night
Of this beautiful house
On Wellington Crescent
That stood so tall
So serene with views
So gorgeous and pleasant

As I climbed the stairs
I had no hopes just fears
As I slowly pushed open his door
I knew he was dead
By the ringing in my head
I didn't need a spirit guide
To know Paul had died
Taken his own life
Death at his own hand and decision
Death by suicide
The first thing I thought in my mind
You silly sod Paul Butters
What about all the great friends who love you
That you've left behind?
His awful looking body vessel
Was an awful bloody sight
But I felt a kind of comfort
Because I knew his gently soul
Has already taken flight
I was not away idling at the races
I was told cops were sent round to check on Paul
Shining their bright lights from torches Into innocents faces
Like talking to a brick wall
They were not the right people sent to check on Paul
Might as well have sent round
A circus clown
He'd dialled the right number
Those cops couldn't have been more dumber than dumber
We have to keep singing the right song
This system of support and caring
Is so – so presently wrong
Shout it out I say from the highest steeple
The importance

Of sending round the right people
Time to take heed
To help people in their dire hour
of desperate need
I sat in the house as quiet as a mouse
His body now gone
Couldn't decipher right from wrong
Full of tears
Full of woe
Too and fro
Thinking did Paul know something
I didn't know
Did he know to leave this rat race
For a far more better more peaceful place
That night I survived suicide
By thinking of my girls
My beauties
And all of my impending
Daddy duties.

The Poets Of SOS
Surviving Suicide

Benjamin Zephaniah was one of the pioneers of the performance poetry scene in Britain. He has spent most of his life performing around the world in schools, universities, concert halls, and other public spaces. His poetry mixes serious issues with humour and is accessible to a wide range of people. He was the first person to record with The Wailers after the death of Bob Marley in a musical tribute to Nelson Mandela, who he later befriended. As well as performing poetry he writes novels, records music, and presents TV and radio programmes. His latest books are *Windrush Child, a novel* for young adults, and *The Life and Rhymes of Benjamin Zephaniah, an autobiography*. He is a visiting professor at De Montfort University, Leicester, and Professor of Poetry and Creative Writing at Brunel University.

Called by the Independent 'British poetry's glam, spangly, shape-shifting answer to David Bowie,' **Jeremy Reed**'s recent collections of poetry include *Piccadilly Bongo, Sooner or Later Frank, Voodoo Excess, Candy4Cannibals, Psychedelic Meadow* and *Dungeness Blues*, together with the non-fiction books, *The Dilly: A Secret History of Piccadilly Rent Boys, Lou Reed Waiting For The Man*, and a recently published London Memoir, *Bandit Poet*. He lives in London and performs as Jeremy Reed and the Ginger Light with the musician Itchy Ear.

James Ragan has authored 10 books (Grove/Atlantic, Henry Holt, Salmon Press, etc) with poems in *Poetry, The Nation, Los Angeles Times, NAR, Epoch, Bomb, Poetry Ireland, World Literature Today* and 30 anthologies. Ragan's honors include 2 Honorary Ph.D's, 3 Fulbright Professorships, Emerson Poetry Prize, 9 Pushcart nominations, a Poetry Society of America Citation, NEA Fellowship, London's Troubadour Prize finalist, the Swan Foundation Humanitarian Award. His plays *Commedia* and *Saints* have been staged in the U.S, Moscow, Beijing, Athens, etc. He's the subject of the documentary "Flowers and Roots," awarded 17 Festival recognitions, including the Platinum Prize at the 49th Houston Film Festival. Currently Distinguished Professor of Poetry at Prague's Charles University.

Tim Tomlinson is the author of *Requiem for the Tree Fort I Set on Fire* (poetry) and *This Is Not Happening to You* (short fiction). Recent work appears in *About Place Journal, Another Chicago Magazine, Litro*, and *Poet Sounds: An Anthology Inspired by the Beach Boys' Pet Sounds*. He is a co-author of New York Writers Workshop's craftbook *The Portable MFA in Creative Writing*, currently in use on four continents. He's a co-founder of New York Writers Workshop, and a professor in NYU's Global Liberal Studies.

Recipient of fellowships and grants from The Rockefeller Foundation, Ireland Literature Exchange, Trubar Foundation, Slovenia, The Institute for the Translation of Hebrew Literature and The Foundation for the Production and Translation of Dutch Literature, **Yuyutsu Sharma** is a Himalayan poet and translator. He has published ten poetry collections including, *The Second Buddha Walk, Space Cake, Amsterdam and Annapurna Poems*. Yuyutsu was at the Poetry Parnassus Festival organized to celebrate London Olympics 2012 where he represented Nepal and India. In 2020, his work was showcased at Royal Kew Gardens in an Exhibit, "Travel the World at Kew." Half the year, he travels and reads all over the world and conducts Creative Writing workshops at various universities in North America and Europe but goes trekking in the Himalayas when back home. Currently, Yuyutsu Sharma edits *Pratik: A Quarterly Magazine of Contemporary Writing.*

Fern Angel Beattie is the founder of independent poetry publishing company, Write Bloody UK. She specializes in what she considers her personal Four Horsemen of the Apocalypse: Women, Love, Sex & Death. Fern has published three poetry collections: *The Trouble With Love* (Lapwing), *Pendulum* (self-published) and *The Art of Shutting Up* (Broken Sleep Books), and has poems in *Belleville Park Pages, The Legendary, JUNGFTAK* and *Blood Tree Literature.* In 2016, she wrote a short film called *Shaping Scars* which was officially selected for LA Dance Short Film Festival, TIFF, Korea Film Festival, L Fest & Flatlands Dance Film Festival. She is also a Fierce Grace hot yoga teacher.

Kirsty Allison's debut novel, *Psychomachia* is published by Wrecking Ball Press. She is the Managing Editor of *Ambit,* founder of Cold Lips, and performs as Vagrant Lovers.

Anne Casey is an award-winning Sydney-based Irish poet and writer. A journalist, magazine editor, legal author and media communications director for 30 years, her work is widely published internationally, ranking in *The Irish Times'* Most Read. Author of the critically acclaimed collections, *out of emptied cups* and *where the lost things go,* she has two new books of poetry forthcoming in 2021. Anne has won poetry awards in Ireland, the UK, the USA, Canada, Hong Kong and Australia. She is the recipient of an Australian Government Scholarship for her PhD in Creative Writing at the University of Technology Sydney.

Originally from Glasgow and now living in South East London, **Gil De Ray** is an artist / musician and filmmaker. He has released 10 albums to date and has performed across the U.K, Europe, America and Japan. He co-edits the literary / art / music / publisher / magazine, *Cold Lips* alongside his partner, Kirsty Allison.

Sadie Maskery in Scotland by the sea with her family. Her writing will be found in 2021 in various places including *British Fantasy Society Horizons, Star*Line, Red Planet Magazine, Odd Magazine, Green Ink, Night Sky Press, Seaborne Magazine, Badlung Press, Cross Crow Keys, The Minison Project, Anser Journal, Fevers of the Mind, Not Very Quiet, Poets Republic, Nightingale and Sparrow, Runcible Spoon,* plus anthologies by the Aequitas Victoria Foundation, Edinburgh Literary Society, Dreich, and 8D Press.

A skateboarder, poet and spoken word artist **Mat Lloyd**'s poetry collaborations with illustrator Matt Frodsham have been featured around the globe. In 2014, he worked with composer Stuart Hancock and the Barbican for their Snapshot Songs Project seeing his work performed by a full choir and the London Schools Symphony Orchestra. His work with Neon Stash x *Stay Wild Magazine, A Guide to Cracks* & *Curbs: London* was widely coveted, seeing it featured on High Snobiety and Tony Hawks Ride channel. In addition, in recent years, he has been featured in the documentary film series, *We Can Fly* and has appeared in the BBC's Skateboarding at 60 documentary.

An artist, playwright, tutor, musician, also a curator and poet, **Eve McDougall** is a consultant and criminal justice advocate public speaker, has spoken in the Houses of Parliament in London and Scotland. Author of *A Wicked Fist: True Story of Prison and Freedom,* over two decades, Eve has worked tirelessly to empower vulnerable people, especially homeless suffering from mental health issues.

Award winning Polish poet, scholar and translator **Dariusz Tomasz Lebioda** has taught at Kazimierz Wielki University for more than three decades. Author of more than seventy books of poetry, short stories, diaries, essays, scientific monographs of European romantic poets and contemporary Polish poets (Miłosz, Herbert, Różewicz, Szymborska) along with world novelists (Faulkner, Caldwell, Golding, Singer, Murdoch, Pahmuk, Coetzee, Naipaul, Lessing, Le Clézio, Mo Yan), Lebioda has won numerous Polish awards including Andrzej Bursa's Award, Stanisław Wyspiański's Award, UNESCO Prize of International Day of Poetry, Ianicius Award, Bruno's Award and Qu Yuan Prize (China 2020). One of the leading poets of the New Generations in Poland – poets born between 1950 and 1960, Lebioda is currently President of European Medal Of Poetry And Art – HOMER.

Sophie Cameron usually performs poetry and rarely appears in print. She ran a cabaret called Red Raw which brought together a variety of challenging live performers. She has started a YouTube channel of short poetry films called Sophie Cameron's After Ours Poetry Dive and can be found on Instagram under Mrs.Franken.Stein

Author of *Rant, Dyslexic me,* **Sam Rapp** (The Dyslexic poet), is an award-winning neuro-diverse writer. She has performed at the Edinburgh Fringe festival 2019, she is a regular on BBC radio Kent. One of her plays about WW1 has been performed in the UK and on TV in Gibraltar. Her second collection is coming out later this year.

Trained as a dancer and a fine artist, **Karen Little** (kazvina) has exhibited her paintings and sculptures internationally. In 2016, her first book, a semi-autobiographical, surrealist novella trilogy, *Filled with Ghosts,* was shortlisted for a Saboteur Award. Her most recent publication remains, *Dissecting an Artist,* an illustrated poetry pamphlet, published by The Black Light Engine Room Press in 2019. She continues to use art and writing as a way of dealing with mental health problems and communicating with people.

Voted in 2019 as the 16th happiest person in England by *The Independent,* **Pat Leacock** (Aka PDLpoet) is a MOBO music award winning composer/multi-instrumentalist as a solo artist and with his groups "The Jazz Steppers" & "Dex & Mercy." He is the co-founder of the hugely popular community radio station, www.hot97uk.com and was a member of a remix group who had a number of UK top 40 chart hits. His monologue poem "The Skin I'm In" has been featured on the London ITV channel's website and SKY TV's "UNMUTED" show.

Ravi Shankar is a Pushcart prize-winning poet, translator and professor who has published over 15 books, including the Muse India award-winning translations, *The Autobiography of a Goddess* and *The Many Uses of Mint: New and Selected Poems 1997-2017.* Along with Tina Chang and Nathalie Handal, he co-edited, *W.W. Norton's Language for a New Century: Contemporary Poetry from the Middle East, Asia & Beyond* called "a beautiful achievement for world literature" by Nobel Laureate Nadine Gordimer. He has taught and performed around the world and appeared in print, radio and TV in such venues as *The New York Times, NPR, BBC* and *the PBS Newshour.* He has won awards to the Corporation of Yaddo and the MacDowell Colony, founded one of the oldest electronic journals of the arts, *Drunken Boat,* and recently finished his PhD from the University of Sydney. His memoir, *Correctional* is forthcoming in 2021 with University of Wisconsin Press.

Yorkshire-born, **Wendy Young** cut her teeth at Survivors Poetry in 2008. Since then she has blogged, reviewed and performed with Disability Arts Online. Her poetry has appeared in *Militant Thistles, Joy of Sound, Poetry Express, Culture Matters, Bread & Roses Anthology 2020, South Bank Poetry; Anomalie Magazine, Magical Women; Together2012 Anthology* and *Persisters Magazine.*

Even at the age of 64, poet **Roy Kirkwood** continues to work at the NHS. He has written poetry most of his life. Only in the last four years, he was able to take his vocation of writing poetry seriously. He used it mainly as a fundraiser for his manuscript and through some small publications of his own was able to raise approximately £5000.

David B. Axelrod is Volusia County, Florida, Poet Laureate (2015-2023). He has been published in fifteen languages and hundreds of magazines and anthologies, and twenty-three books of poetry, most recently *Mother Tongue*. Dr. Axelrod is recipient of three Fulbright Awards including his being the first official Fulbright Poet-in-Residence in the People's Republic of China. He is publisher of Writers Ink Press. He lives in Daytona Beach where he is the founder/director of Creative Happiness Institute, Inc., a not-for-profit organization presenting programs in creative writing and alternative wellness.

Sydney-born, **Megan Garrett-Jones** is a performance artist and writer living by the Kent seaside. She hosts Things with Words, 'expanded poetry' events which have been programmed by POW!. She was a poet-in-residence at Dreamland for Margate Now, for which she appeared as a mermaid with a vintage typewriter, collecting people's dreams and turning them into poems. Megan is currently working on a one-woman show wrestling with contemporary feminism, call Femme Fantastic: the spoken word musical.

Netherlands-born, **Judith Mok** has authored two novels and three poetry collections in Dutch, a novel and a poetry Collection in English. Her short stories have been short listed twice for the Francis Mc Manus award and her first novel, *The innocents at the Circus,* has been written in French for the Prix de l'Academie Francaise which led to a three day visit to the Academie. Her work has appeared nationally and internationally in numerous literary magazines and anthologies. She has been supported by the Irish Arts council. Recently, in December 2016, Judith received a Patrick Kavanagh fellowship. Judith Mok travels the world as a classical singer and vocal coach.

Sandra Yannone's poems and book reviews have appeared in numerous print and online journals including *Ploughshares, Poetry Ireland Review, Prairie Schooner, Sweet, The Blue Nib, Live Encounters, Impossible Archetype,* and *Lambda Literary Review.* Her poem "Requiem for Orlando" appeared in *Pulsamos: LGBTQ Poets Respond to the Pulse Nightclub Shooting,* a special online edition of *Glass: A Journal of Poetry* in August, 2016. Salmon Poetry published her debut collection *Boats for Women* in 2019 and will publish *The Glass Studio* in 2022. She currently hosts Cultivating Voices LIVE Poetry on Facebook via Zoom on Sundays.

Bill Wolak is an American poet, collagist, and photographer who has just published his eighteenth book of poetry entitled, *All the Wind's Unfinished Kisses* with Ekstasis Editions.

Madeleine White was born in Germany, with roots in Canada and the UK. A magazine publisher and editor, she has produced national and international web and print magazines, creating a voice for those without one, such as the successful Nina-Iraq, a project she worked on with the World Bank to reach Iraqi women everywhere. Her debut novel *Mother Of Floods* was published by Crowsnest Books in 2020 and her poetry and audio drama have been successfully published and performed across a number of national and international platforms. Since 2019, she has been founder/editor of *Write On!* magazine and *Write On! Extra e-zine,* published by Pen to Print, an Arts Council NPO organisation.

Christopher Southgate trained originally as a biochemist, and has since been a house-husband, a bookseller, a lay chaplain in university and mental health settings, and a teacher of theology. He has published four collections on poetry with Shoestring Press, the most recent being *Chasing the Raven* (2016). In 1997 he wrote an exploration of the life of T.S. Eliot through an extended biographical poem with companion essays, published as *A Love and its Sounding* (Salzburg). In 2017 Canterbury Press brought out an edition of Southgate's spiritual poems entitled, *Rain falling by the River.* His theological work includes *The Groaning of Creation,* which has proved to be a seminal study of the problem of suffering in evolution. Chris lives on the edge of Dartmoor, Devon, and he continues to be deeply influenced by this landscape, as well as by the journey of his Christian faith.

Patricia Carragon's fiction piece *What Has to Happen Next* has been nominated for Sundress Publications Annual Best of the Net Anthology. Her poem *Paris the Beautiful* won Poem of the Week from *great weather for MEDIA*. She was nominated by Bear Creek Haiku for a Pushcart Prize. Her latest books from Poets Wear Prada are *Meowku* and *The Cupcake Chronicles* and her debut novel, *Angel Fire*, is from Alien Buddha Press. Patricia hosts Brownstone Poets and is the editor-in-chief of its annual anthology. She is an executive editor for *Home Planet News Online*. She lives in Brooklyn, NY.

Karen Corinne Herceg graduated from Columbia University where she majored in Literature and Writing. She is a recipient of New York State grants and has featured at major venues with such renowned poets as John Ashbery and Philip Schultz. She writes poetry, essays, reviews, and fiction for both U.S. and international publications. Her second book of poems, *Out From Calaboose*, was released by Nirala in 2017. She resides in France.

David Noone was born in Ireland, spending his childhood in a rural village in Co Kildare. His novel, *Saint of the City*, has been praised by novelist Cathi Unsworth and musician Gavin Friday. He continues to live and write in Dublin.

Gill Fewins was born and grew up in South East London. Gill lives in Kent and works as a Registered Manager for a fostering agency. She has written three books, and loves writing poetry, some of which has featured on radio Kent. She has an amazing husband, two grown up sons and five beautiful grandchildren.

Michael Graves is an American poet, editor, and Instructor of English at the City University of New York. Mike is the author of *A Prayer for the Less Violent Offenders: New & Selected Short Poems*, and *Adam and Cain*, and moderator of the Phoenix Reading Series in NYC which he founded in 1995.

Catherine Alice Woods is a newcomer to poetry. Her first poem *Little Yellow Tree* was written during the second lockdown, and she has been writing daily since. After spending several years in Germany and Italy teaching English, Catherine has returned to the UK to study social work as she wants to help support local communities. Recently, she has been working alongside the Time to Talk Befriending charity on their *Staying Together, Recovering Together* research project and is an outreach volunteer for Yada - an organisation supporting self-identifying women in the sex industry.

John Prastitis' poems were first published in collections such as *West Country Now*, whilst living in Bristol. He also contributed to Bristol University magazine, *The Heckier*, played in a couple of bands , DJed and helped organize gigs and clubs mainly as part of the Kronstadt Klub. After a year on a foundation art course, he moved back to London to study a fine art degree at Camberwell College of art. He has exhibited paintings in Bristol, London and Margate, most recently prison to pavement while homeless for a year. He has worked for Saneline Mental Health Charity and Arnolfini Art Gallery in Bristol. He lives in Margate.

Agnes Marton is a Hungarian-born poet, writer, librettist, Fellow of the Royal Society of Arts (UK), and reviews editor at The Ofi Press. Recent publications include her collection *Captain Fly's Bucket List* and four chapbooks with Moria Books (USA). She has been a resident poet at the Scott Polar Research Institute at the University of Cambridge, on a research boat in the Arctic Circle, and also in Iceland, Italy, Ireland, Serbia, Portugal, Chile, Canada and the United States. She is based in Luxembourg.

Suzanne French has worked in the fashion and entertainment industry for over 10 years. Due to the pandemic and close family suffering with mental health issues that have been heightened by it, she has explored poetry as an artistic outlet.

Rory Paddle (RawbyNature) is a creative free spirit hailing from the south of England, bounced back and forth between Brighton and country bumpkin. Rapper, spoken-worder, Poet, Singer and guitar-hugging instrumental dabbler. A published Writer who "loves all decent and originally pioneered music". "I strive to push boundaries; blend genres into new sounds. I hope my tales inspire people, give them a little solace, a little spark; occasionally a BIG smile. That's art, right?" As well as his fixation in pioneering through creative integrity, Raw's motivations are people, global unification and conservation. This has seen his work broadcasted by the likes of BBC6 Music and Radio Reverb. He has collaborated with Keith Lavene, project Haiflu (featured on BBC Radio 4) and PEN International – as well as contributing to the world's longest online poetry event. He continues to be a presence in thescene and is performing at Kaya Festival this August.

DPart is a chart topping rapper from North West London. His Mother died when he was seven. He suffers with mental health issues that he confronts face on with his music.

Dave Mankind is a singer, poet, occultist and former herb vendor from Barnsley, South Yorkshire, England.

Timothy Gager is the author of sixteen books of fiction and poetry. His latest, *2020 Poems*, is his ninth of poetry, and was a #1 Bestseller on Amazon. Timothy hosted the successful Dire Literary Series in Cambridge, Massachusetts from 2001 to 2018, and as a virtual series starting in 2020.

Recipient of numerous awards, **Carlotta Allum** is a practitioner, researcher and director and founder of the arts charity *Stretch* that works with prisoners and vulnerable groups in society. Her research is with the Design Against Crime Research Centre and Socially Responsive Design Hub who invited her to work with them after working with her on some storytelling work within their Makeright Project. Carlotta founded *Stretch* as a result of her MA in Museums and Galleries in Education from the Institute of Education, UCL and has since been awarded research scholarships for work with prisoners from the Griffins Society, LSE and the Winston Churchill Memorial Trust, where she travelled to Norway and Australia. Her practice was originally grounded in museology and using objects for stories where she worked with the V&A and Welcome Trust amongst other high profile partners.

Anna Halberstadt grew up in Lithuania and was trained as a psychologist at Moscow University and in the U.S.. Widely published poet and translator, she has published several collections including *Vilnius Diary* and *Green in a Landscape with Ashes*, and *Transit and Gloomy Sun*. She is a recipient of the International Merit Award by *Atlanta Review*. Her new book of Selected Poems in Lithuanian translation, *Transit*, was named one of TOP15 poetry books of 2020 by Lt.15.

Agnes Meadows is studying for an MA in Psychoanalytic Studies at Birkbeck, University of London. She has a forthcoming article in the History Workshop Journal about a letter from Anna Freud that she came across while volunteering in the Freud Archive. When she is not writing, reading or knitting, Agnes is a primary school teaching assistant.

Yogesh Patel has received an MBE for literature. He has co-edited *Skylark* magazine since 1969. Currently, he runs Skylark Publications UK and the Word Masala Foundation. Honoured with Freedom of the City of London, he has LP records, films, radio, children's book, fiction, non-fiction books, and three poetry collections to his credit. In 2019, he was a Poet-of-Honor at New York University. The House of Lords and the National Poetry Library have staged his readings. Amidst many, *PN Review, The London Magazine*, and BBC TV and Radio have published his work. So have also numerous anthologies, including National Curriculum, MacMillan, Sahitya Akademi and others.

Gerard Beirne has published two collections of poetry and 4 books of prose. Hennessy New Irish Writer of the Year Award winner, shortlisted for the Danuta Gleed Literary Award, Bord Gais Irish Book Awards, and Kerry Group Irish Fiction Award. He lectures in Creative Writing at IT Sligo and regularly facilitates Writing and Wellness workshops.

Carol Lynn Stevenson Grellas lives is currently enrolled in the Vermont College of Fine Arts', MFA in Writing program. She is an eleven-time Pushcart

Prize nominee and a seven-time Best of the Net nominee. In 2012 she won the Red Ochre Chapbook Contest, with her manuscript, *Before I Go to Sleep*. In 2018, her book *In the Making of Goodbyes* was nominated for The CLMP Firecracker Award in Poetry. In 2019, her chapbook *An Ode to Hope in the Midst of Pandemonium* was a category finalist for the Eric Hoffer Book Award. Her latest collection of poems *Alice in Ruby Slippers* is newly released from Aldrich Press. She has severed as editor for both *the Orchards Poetry Journal* and *the Tule Review*.

Megha Sood is a Pushcart-nominated Poet, Editor, and Blogger from New Jersey. Her work has appeared in *Poetry Society of New York, American Writers Review, Rising Phoenix Review, Kissing Dynamite*, etc. National Level Winner Spring Mahogany Lit Prize 2020 and Three-Time State-level winner of NJ Poetry Contest 2018/2019/2020. Two books of her poetry, *My Body is Not an Apology* and *My Body Lives Like a Threat* shall appear later this year.

A Nepali poet and fiction writer of younger generation, **Amar Aakash** (Laxman Adhikari) contributes columns to several Nepalese newspapers and journals, including leading literary monthly, *Madhuparka*. His debut collection of short stories is due in 2021. Adhikari lives in Kathmandu.

Tim Kahl is the author of five books of poems, the latest a collection of sijo called CALIFORNIA SIJO where 53 of the sijo have been set to music. He is also editor of *Clade Song*. He plays flutes, guitars, ukuleles, charangos and cavaquinhos. He currently teaches at California State University, Sacramento, where he sings lieder while walking on campus between classes.

A 2020 nominee for Best of the Web, widely published poet **Carrie Magness Radna** is an audiovisual cataloger at New York Public Library, a singer, a lyricist-songwriter. She recently won an Honorable Mention Award for "all trains are haunted" in the 89th annual *Writer's Digest* Writer's Competition (Non-Rhyming Poetry). She has published two poetry collections, *Hurricanes never apologize* (Luchador Press, 2019) and *In the blue hour* (Nirala, 2021). Born in Norman, Oklahoma, she currently lives with her husband Rudolf in Manhattan.

Simon Miles is a former journalist who currently works on the journalism programme at The University of East London. Some time back, he co-ran the influential live arts cabaret The Cupboard off Oxford Street which amongst other things showcased the outsider end of performance. At roughly the same time he worked as writer-in-residence at a couple of prisons, and during that period met Dean Stalham with whom he shares a commitment to supporting the work of emergent artists.

Henry Madd is a competition winning poet who has performed across the UK and internationally. After winning the Apples and Snakes Emerging Artist Award in 2017, he went on to become two-time Kent Slam Champion. Henry is committed to delivering successful community art projects that encourage people to connect with the place they call home and he facilitates creative workshops for the arts charity 'Create'. Henry regularly hosts and produces music and poetry events around Kent, including 'Bramleys Sessions' YouTube Channel, and is a supported artist of The Marlowe.

Luke Sullivan has faced the highs and lows of living. Times of homelessness and wayward paths have sent him on a journey to make himself and others become the best version of themselves. He is a family man with high morals and fearless motivation. Living with ADHD, Depression and a fundamental thirst for philosophy, Luke has grown into an honourable authentic man, who shows compassion for others. Luke grew up in the skateboarding scene in and around London. He is now director of The Far Skate Foundation - helping young people in education alongside skateboarding to gain engagement. He is governor of two primary schools, ran in local elections and is in the process of building an Olympic skateboarding training centre. Luke proves that the only limits to success are the barriers we set ourselves.

Acknowledgments

Thank you, firstly, to all the poets and their contributions. Thanks you to Malcolm Allum for his work on the formatting and Rosalind Allum for her encouragement. Thank you to the Arts Council for their continued support of the work of Stretch and Dean Stalham. Thank you to all at Nirala Publications for their hard work and support. Special thanks to Kirsty Allison for her words of encouragement also.

Thank you to all who read this book and spread its sentiments

Nirala Series

A Series of Contemporary Writing

Kailash: Jewel of the Snows
Rajinder Arora
ISBN: 978-8193936719 Paperback 2021 pp 268
plus 68 color Demy

A Short History of Nepal
From Ancient to Modern Times
Shreeram Prasad Upadhyaya
ISBN 9-788182-500174 2021 PP 255

Mother's Hand: Selected Poems
A Bilingual English/Nepali Anthology
by **Jidi Majia**
Translated into Nepali by **Yuyutsu RD Sharma**
ISBN: 978-8182500174 Paperback pp 96 Demy

Dancing in Place: *New Poems*
S. Renay Sanders
ISBN ISBN 81-8250-048-6 2019 pp. 64 Paper Demy

Blue Fan Whirring: *Poems*
Mike Jurkovic
ISBN 978-8182500969 2019 pp. 160 Paper

The Second Buddha Walk:
Inspired by The Second Buddha ,
Master of Time Exhibit at Rubin Museum, New York
Yuyutsu Sharma
ISBN 978-8182500983 2019 pp. 52 Paper Demy

Imagined Secrets: *New Poems*
Robert Scotto
ISBN 978-81825000442019 pp. 79 Paper Demy

The Tin Man
David B. Austell
ISBN 9-788182-500792 2019 pp.320 Hard Demy

All Vows: : *New & Selected Poems*
David B. Axelrod
ISBN 978-8182500822 2016 pp 194

The Dhimals: Miraculous Migrants of Himal:
An Anthropological Study of a Nepalese Ethnic Group
Rishikeshab Raj Regmi
ISBN 9788182500082 2016 PP 294

Path to Excellence: : *A Memoir by India's Distinguished Academician*
Pritam B. Sharma
ISBN : 81-8250-0907 2017 Hard Cover pp 358

Word Has It, Poems
Ruth Danon
ISBN 81-8250-097-4 2018 Paperback pp 85

Eternal Snow: *A Worldwide Anthology of One Hundred Twenty Five   Poetic Intersections with Himalayan Poet Yuyutsu RD Sharma*
Edited by **David Austell & Kathleen D Gallagher**
ISBN : 81-8250-088-5 2017 Paperback pp 309

Cats, Love & Other Surprises
by **Otis Kidwell Burger**, Illustrations by Katherine Burger
ISBN : 978-8182500891 2017 Hardback pp 65 RS. 1495

Letters from a Sacred Mountain Place:
A Journey through the Nepal Himalayas –
Photographs and Text by **Diane Frank**
ISBN 81-8250-095-8 2018 Hard Cover pp 144

Making of The Indian Muse
Context and Perspectives in Indian Poetry in English
Edited by **Goutam Karmakar**
ISBN 978-8182500273 2019 pp 430

Ritual: The Magical Perspective : *Efficacy an the Search for Inner Meaning*
Luc Sala
ISBN 9-788182-500617 2014 Hard pp.832

A Blizzard In My Bones: New York Poems
Yuyutsu RD Sharma
ISBN 81-8250-070-2 2016 pp.134 Paper

Inside the Shell of the Tortoise
Poems written in India and Nepal : *A Spanish English Edition*
Veronica Aranda
Translated by **Claudia Routon** with **Yuyutsu Sharma**
ISBN 9-788182-500686 2016 pp.56 Hard

Your Kiss is a River : *Poems of Love, Food and Life*
Carolyn Wells
ISBN 9-788182-500532 2016 pp.56 Hard

Space Cake, Amsterdam
& Other Poems from Europe and America
Yuyutsu RD Sharma
ISBN-81-8250-059-1 2014 Hard pp. 110

Milarepa's Bones, Helambu : *33 New Poems*
Yuyutsu RD Sharma
ISBN-81-8250-032-X 2012 Hard pp.64

Little Creek *& Other Poems*
David Austell
ISBN 81-8250- 031-1 2011 Hard pp.200

The Mystery Over Lord Buddha's Roots
An Analysis of the Mystery of the Shakya Kingdom
Mitsuaki KOJIMA
ISBN 9-788182-500563 2014 Hard pp.165

TEN: The New Indian Poets
Selected and Edited by **Jayanta Mahapatra & Yuyutsu Sharma**
ISBN 9-788182-500341 2012 pp.134 Hard

Dada Poetry :*An Introduction* by **William Seaton**
Foreword by **Timothy Shipe**
ISBN-9-788182-500358 2013 Hard pp.112

Libraries, Information Centers &
Information Professionalism in Nepal by Madhusudan Karki
ISBN 9-788182-500372 2012 Hard pp.348

The Yeti : Spirit of Himalayan Forest Shamans by Larry G. Peters
ISBN 9-788182-500525 2014 Hard pp.128

Folk Tales of Sherpa and Yeti
Collected by **Shiva Dhakal,** *Adapted by* **Yuyutsu RD Sharma**
ISBN 9-788182-500624 2014 Paper pp.125

Annapurnas & Stains of Blood:*Life, Travel & Writing on a page of Snow*
Yuyutsu RD Sharma
ISBN 9-788182-500129 2010 Hard pp.200

Trance, Initiation & Psychotherapy in Nepalese Shamanism
Essays on Tamang and Tibetan Shamanism by **Larry G. Peters**
ISBN 9-788182-500532 2014 Paper pp.412

Tamang Shamans :
An Ethnopsychiatric Study of Ecstasy and Healing in Nepal
Larry G. Peters ISBN 9-788182-500099 2007 Paper pp.179

The Pokhara Valley : *A Traveler's Guide by* **LB Thapa**
ISBN 9-788182-500198 2010 Paper pp.202

Ocean in a Drop: *Yoga, Meditation and Life in the Himalayas*
Swami Chandresh
ISBN 81-8250- 005-2 2006 Hard pp.348

The Price of Heaven *Travel Stories from India and Nepal*
Evald Flisar
Translated from Slovene by **the Author & Alan McConnell-Duff**
ISBN 81-8250- 020-6 2009 Paper pp.140

Student Politics & Democracy in Nepal by Meena Ojha
ISBN 9-788182-500259 2010 Hard pp.411

WHITE LOTUS BOOKS

I Choose to Cry and Love You:
Maile Roje Runa Ra Timilai Maya Garna
(A Bilingual English/Nepali)
Yang Qingxiang Translated into the Nepali by Yuyutsu Sharma
ISBN: 978-9937079013 Paperback 2021 pp355 Dem

Ek Asadharan Antarvarta: Flash Fiction
by Lao Ma Translated into Nepali by Yuyutsu Sharma
ISBN: 978-9937-0-7902-0 Paperback 2021 pp 334 Demy

Panaharu Khalichan : Kavitaka Dui Dashak (Poems)
Yuyustu R.D. Sharma
ISBN 81-8250-004-4 2020 Paper pp. 140

Bhojpure Hulakiko Santaan, Atamgat (A Memoir)
Shailendra Sakar ISBN: 978-9937056526 Paperback 2021 pp 209 Demy

Nachganko Rajdhani Bhaktapur:
(Bhaktapur A City of Music & Dance)
Jagadish Rana ISBN 978-8182500433 Hardcover 2011 pp 84

Nirdoshharuko Nyaya ra anya Kavitaharu by David B. Austell
ISBN 9789937056533 pp.40 2015 Paperback

EPSILONMEDIA BOOKS

Annapurna, Everest, Helambu & Langtang : Mini Nepal Trilogy
Poetry by Yuyutsu RD Sharma, *Photographs* by Andreas Stimm
ISBN: 978-3981088342 Hardcover 2015 pp 200

The Nepal Trilogy Part I-III Annapurna, Everest,
Helambu & Langtang
Hasselblad XPan photographs & Poetryfrom the main trekking
areas of Nepal. www.Nepal-Trilogy.de,
English-german ISBN: ISBN 978-3-9810883-2-8)
Paperback Box 2015 pp 800